94 Declared

BEN TRAVERS

94 Declared

CRICKET REMINISCENCES

★

Foreword by Brian Johnston

ELM TREE BOOKS
London

First published in Great Britain 1981
by Elm Tree Books/Hamish Hamilton Ltd
Garden House 57–59 Long Acre London WC2E 9JZ

Copyright © 1981 The Literary Executors of Ben Travers

British Library Cataloguing in Publication Data

Travers, Ben
    94 declared.
    1. Cricket—History—20th century
    I. Title
    796.35'8'0924   GV913
    ISBN 0–241–10591–9

Printed in Great Britain by
Bristol Typesetting Co. Ltd,
Barton Manor, St Philips, Bristol

CONTENTS

ILLUSTRATIONS

ACKNOWLEDGEMENTS

The publishers would like to thank the following for their kind permission to reproduce their pictures :

The Press Association : Percy Chapman, George Gunn, Jack Hobbs, Douglas Jardine, Alan Kippax, Sir Pelham Warner.

The Marylebone Cricket Club : Larwood, J. M. Gregory and line illustration of W. G. Grace in text.

Central Press Photos Ltd : Alan Davidson, Patsy Hendren.

BBC Hulton Picture Library : A. C. MacLaren.

David Frith : Ben Travers and 1930 Australian Cricketers, the Kippax Incident and line illustrations in the text on pages 2, 12, 20.

Associated Newspapers Group Limited for the two Tom Webster cartoons reproduced in the text.

Especial thanks are due to Brian Johnston and David Frith for their invaluable help in tracing suitable illustrations.

FOREWORD

I shall remember forever, with great relish, the Saturday of the Lord's Test Match against the West Indians in 1980. On the Saturday of each Test we always invite someone to our commentary box on *Test Match Special* to talk to us for half an hour during the luncheon interval. The only qualification they need, no matter what their profession or job, is that they should love cricket. They needn't even have played it, which inevitably means that they are, or have been, watchers.

For Saturday, 22 June, someone, probably our producer Peter Baxter, had the bright idea of inviting Ben Travers who, at 94 years old, was certainly the oldest living watcher, spanning Test Matches from 1896 to 1980. I personally was delighted at the prospect. As a schoolboy on my way back to Eton I always had to pass through London. I was given extra pocket money for lunch before catching the train for Windsor, but, for at least five years, I settled for a sandwich and put the money towards a seat at the Aldwych matinée to see one of Ben's famous farces. I was lucky enough to catch *Rookery Nook, Thark, Plunder, A Cup of Kindness, A Night Like This* and *Turkey Time*. Then years later when, after the war, I had become a cricket commentator with the BBC, I met Ben in person on the cricket circuit, either at Tests in this country or on tours abroad. He was always the same : a bird-like figure with sharp twinkling eyes, bubbling with enthusiasm, sparkling wit and an unquenchable thirst for knowledge about anything to do with cricket.

Those of us who knew him were confident that he would give a superb performance. But we were naturally concerned as to how he would cope with a large Saturday crowd, and how at, his age, he would be able to climb up to our commentary box right at the top of the pavilion. There are 79 steps, and for years John Arlott has counted and cursed them. But we need not have worried. We sent a car to collect him from his flat near Baker Street, and he arrived at about 1.10 pm with the commentary still going on. Inspite of the climb, he looked as spritely and perky as ever and in no way distressed. We sat him down in a corner seat and gave him a glass of champagne which we knew was his favourite tipple and which we just happened to have in the box. Somehow or other he managed to keep quiet whilst play continued until 1.30 pm; there then followed a short summary of the morning's cricket, before we returned to the studio for a news bulletin.

I usually preside over these lunch-time sessions, and with me on this occasion were John Arlott and Trevor Bailey. When Dick Maddock in the studio handed back to us at 1.40 pm, I briefly introduced Ben in what I hope were welcoming and felicitous terms—and then it was just like turning on a tap. I only had to put one question to him and he was off on a magic memory tour of Test cricket, starting with the very first Test he saw at the Oval in 1896. We all sat in amazed and wondering silence. It was a fabulous performance. Without a single note he seemed to be re-living every detail of what he had seen. He described players of the past—their appearance, characters and style—plus, in many cases, the exact way in which they had been dismissed or had bowled out an opponent.

All that was needed from me was the occasional 'prompt' question to steer him on to the next period of his cricketing life—otherwise he might have gone on until tea-time and we only had half an hour. I know that Trevor Bailey never asked a single question, and John Arlott, I think, only one. It was a virtuoso memory act which no one I know could possibly have matched. It only stopped when the players were back on the field, ready to restart after lunch, and it was time to resume commentary. We had been so enthralled that we had even abandoned our usual lunch-time cricket scoreboard at 2.05 pm.

Whilst we sat there, silently applauding Ben, he seemed completely unmoved and unaware of the effect his performance had had on all of us. He listened to the commentary while he had a bite to eat and then, at about 2.30 pm, silently bade everyone good-bye. I went down with him to the back of the pavilion, where a taxi was waiting to take him back to his flat. I thanked him profusely and was delighted that he seemed to have enjoyed the broadcast so much himself. That was the last time I saw Ben.

Thankfully Michael Brown and Roger Houghton of Elm Tree Books heard the broadcast and were sufficiently inspired to ask Ben to put it all down in this book. And, typically, he delivered the complete script typed by himself right on time four months later. I am sure that, like all of us in the commentary box, you will be amazed at his fantastic memory and be enchanted by his tremendous enthusiasm and sense of fun. As I said earlier, in the broadcast he never used a single note. On the day before he died I received a charming letter from him in which he recalled his enjoyment of the broadcast and apologised for any slight inaccuracies there might be in the text of the book. He had not had a single *Wisden* to help him— just a few old cricket magazines, mostly Australian. A truly remarkable and entirely loveable man.

The title of this book was to have been '94 Not Out'. Alas Ben did not reach the 'coveted three figures', but as a cricket lover he would know that, so far as the team is concerned, a score in the nineties is as good as a hundred. Well played Ben.

BRIAN JOHNSTON

INTRODUCTION

They sent him in to open the innings for Surrey at the Oval, the paternal figure of old Tom Hayward accompanied him to the wicket. It was the young chap's first appearance in first-class cricket, but he soon made it look less of an ordeal for himself than for the bowlers. I watched him play a delightful innings of 88. J. B. Hobbs.

They sent him in at number five or six on Sydney cricket ground to confront, or rather to assault, English bowlers for the first time in his career. Those English bowlers had heard a good deal in advance about the boy wonder from Bowral and they soon realised that they were destined to hear a great deal more. I watched him make a brilliant 67 in quick time. D. G. Bradman.

On both occasions, I felt like some watcher of the skies when a new planet swims into his ken. And, with all respect to John Keats, I would rather have acquired that feeling my way than by having to read Chapman's Homer.

Watcher is the key word. Books by the hundred have been written about cricket; by judges, critics, connoisseurs, theorists and commentators, to say nothing of the records of their own careers vouchsafed to us by many gifted exponents of the game. The bookshelves of the dedicated cricket lover are crammed with these volumes; he has to keep a separate set of shelves for his collection of Wisden's Almanacs. Can he possibly find room to squeeze in yet another little cricket book? I hope he may do so. But why should he? For two reasons.

Firstly, it occurred to somebody (Brian Johnston, I think) that I, purely in my capacity as a watcher, should broadcast a radio talk during the luncheon interval on the Saturday of the 1980 Test Match at Lord's. But why pick on me? Because I was the oldest watcher in the business. When my hour arrived, the first question put to me was: 'When did you start watching cricket?' My reply: 'My first Test Match was at the Oval in 1896,' caused a general little gasp of surprise and some almost incredulous eyebrow-work. And, after all, there cannot be many old boys still knocking around who saw W. G. Grace make a century or G. L. Jessop's historic 104 in the Oval England v. Australia Test Match of 1902.

The commentators at Lord's are boxed into a narrow eyrie above the pavilion. There is only room for four of them to sit alongside each other in the front line. When I arrived, Fred Trueman, awaiting his turn to succeed Trevor Bailey, jumped up and insisted, amid a good deal of whispered argument, on surrendering his seat to me and John Arlott brought me a glass of Moët. The glass of Moët may have proved beneficial and, once having dealt graphically with the scene of Jessop's innings, I swept ahead, borne on the tide of reminiscence, drifting occasionally into generalities of a lightsome nature.

The commentators expressed themselves well satisfied with Brian Johnston's gamble and I went away with a feeling of relief at having at any rate filled the bill without any egregious mishap. Then, greatly to my gratified surprise, I learned that my babble had tickled the fancy not only of the bunched-up occupants of the eyrie but of those of the public of all ages, sizes and sexes who happened to have been listening in. So much so that the programme was repeated by request during the ensuing Test Match at Old Trafford.

Apparently what had caught and held the attention of the old cricket devotee, and of his successors, was to be given an actual eye-witness's account of W.G. and his contemporaries and of the Jessop miracle. So this is my primary reason for letting them have a somewhat elaborated version of the same in print. Self-assertion? Actuated by a feeling of cockiness at being so old as to be able to patronise my cricket-loving juniors with recollections which none of them can share? Oh, but I am told they were keen to hear them and, if so, they may also like to leave those years behind and to join, or rejoin, me in the considerably later vintage period of the late 1920s and early 1930s. For it was during that time that I had the good fortune to get to know all of England's and Australia's Test Match players, their personalities and utterances; some of the latter reserved for my own special benefit. Needless to say, I witnessed many remarkable performances and incidents on the field of play in this Hobbs, Bradman, Hammond heyday. To recall some of them may prove irresistible, but my chief objective is to allocate my recollections backstage.

One

Start of the Innings

How it all came about—these few paradisiacal years in a cricket-lover's lifetime—was undreamt of until it actually started in the autumn of 1928; a generation later than that day, 10 August 1896, when a little boy of nine sat with his father at the Vauxhall end of Kennington Oval at his first Test Match.

Whatever great changes cricket may have undergone during the past century, it remained exactly as it is today in one respect—the start was delayed by rain. It subsided into drizzle, then stopped; but the ground and in particular the pitch had to be given time to dry out—and given an exasperating length of time. You may picture my childish restlessness, kicking my boots about—'Oh, why can't they start?' I remember so well my kind father's practical, consolatory cheerfulness (he was an outspoken man): 'They soon will. Cheer up, it's only tea time. Let's pump-ship and have a bun.'

Then, at last, out came the umpires; out came G. H. S. Trott leading the Australian side and then—a great moment and one which still remains a great moment eighty-four years later—my first sight of W.G.

All the tedium of the wasted hours melted into thin air. There he was with that beard and striped cap which hitherto I had seen and revered only in photographs. He was accompanied by F. S. Jackson, but never mind anybody else for the present, though it may perhaps be as well to record the list of names which appeared on my already well-thumbed and dilapidated score-card: W. G. Grace, F. S. Jackson, K. S. Ranjitsinhji, Abel (R), A. C. MacLaren, Hayward (T), E. G. Wynyard, Peel

British Pluck.
The Crowd sitting out the
Deluge of Monday.

Read Tablets
all the best.

G. Giffen
bowling.

Lady
The Australian
Giant.

Removing the roller.

"The Doctor" wins the Toss
from Trott.

More Pain.

Trumble.

Kumar Shri
Ranjitsinhji

Trott gets out Grace
by an easy catch
at Point.

Craig "The Poet"
says a few words about
the strike.

2

(R), Lilley (A.A.), Hearne (J. T.), Richardson (T). Note the differentiation made at that time and for many years to come between Gentlemen and Players. The pros were only allowed to emerge and make their valuable contributions from a separate and secondary gate. The segregated amateurs were alleged to offer their services free of charge; though it was also always said that W.G. employed his own methods of getting round that.

I was, of course, too young to realise that this was to be one of those matches when to win the toss and take first innings was to win the game at the outset if the weather held good for the next two days, which it did. Jackson, who was substituting for A. E. Stoddart, injured, put up a useful partnership with Grace, but Grace himself was caught by Trott at point when he had made 24. Jackson carried his score to 45, which was to be the second highest innings in the match. During the two following days the drying wicket gave Hearne and Peel for England and Trumble for Australia all the answers to slow bowlers' prayers. In the fourth innings Australia made 44 all told (Hearne 6 for 23, Peel 4 for 19) and I sat, spanking my knees in triumph, as the wickets fell. Their number eleven batsman, one McKibbin, alone slogged his way into double figures. I well remember his finally snicking the ball to Bobby Abel at first slip, Abel collaring the ball and in one and the same movement making a dash with it to the pavilion. I also particularly recall two catches made in the long field by Mac-Laren. They were probably pretty straightforward catches but to me, at the time, it seemed a stupendous feat to be able to hold on to a ball which steeped to and from the distant heights. It is curious how certain specific incidents implant themselves in the mind of a nine-year-old cricket watcher. I recall, too, the crowd bursting into song on Ranji's appearance from the pavilion.

But to have seen W.G. was no mere incident; it was a great occasion in my young life. He was bowled by Trumble for 9 in

3

England's second innings and that was his farewell to Test cricket. But I was to see him again some three or four times in the years that immediately followed. Towards the end of his

TO THE BOUNDARY.

career he forsook Gloucestershire and formed a club of his own, which he named London County with Headquarters at the Crystal Palace, playing home and away matches which were included in the first-class fixture list against various counties. I suppose he kept some sort of staff attached to London County but, if so, it must have been a very skeleton staff, for his system was to rope in all the best players he could lay his hands on who were not engaged in a county match at the time.

So, one day, a year or two after that Oval match, I journeyed from my home in Bromley, Kent, to the Crystal Palace to watch the opening day of London County v. Surrey. Another red-letter day in my years of Grace—and surely the reddest. For I watched him make a century in partnership with Ranji, who also made one on his own. I was favoured by good fortune and so was W.G., because he looked to be out when he had made only about 20, caught at short leg by Brockwell, who was incidentally a top-class all-rounder, in and out of the England sides. Brockwell threw the ball up triumphantly, but W.G. made violent gestures intimating that he had hit a bump-ball and then advanced towards Brockwell, brandishing his bat as if to fell him. He looked very formidable but perhaps it was merely his good-natured way of indicating that he wished to go on batting. This, with the umpire remaining intimidated and mute, the great man proceeded to do with the result that I have ever since been able to boast that I saw him make one of his many hundreds. I wonder how many people can say the same.

I was to see him again during a Hastings Festival and yet again when the gentlemen of England played an opening-of-the-season match against Surrey at the Oval. It was in this match that I first caught sight of Jack Hobbs playing that initial first-class innings I have mentioned—first-class in every sense. As Hobbs himself was to inform me, many years later, he and the old master coincided on only two occasions in the cricket field and to have seen, as I did, W. G. Grace bowling (round-arm) to Hobbs—did I realise at the time that I was witnessing a landmark in the history of cricket?

W.G., I picture him still in his stance at the wicket : the left foot with the heel planted and the toe cocked up, the bat held with both hands together high on the handle and with the base immobile a few inches from the crease as he awaited the on-coming bowler. Apart from his remarkable and unmistakable physical appearance, the substantial (to be polite) frame, the beard, the inevitable cap, it was his whole pre-eminent personality that dominated, as no individual before or since has dominated, the scene. I like to think that he remains and always will remain the accredited and traditional daddy of the game.

Like G. K. Chesterton, another man of considerable bulk, he possessed a surprisingly high, almost a falsetto, tone of voice. Another generally unrecognised fact is that on and off during his cricket career he continued to remind himself and his patients that he was a qualified medical practitioner. It will be remembered (no, of course, it won't) that the more meticulous or servile of cricket reporters always referred to him as *Dr* W. G. Grace. My mother, who was born and brought up in Clifton, told me that she remembered him visiting the house in the role of the family doctor. I have been guilty of the comment that none of the family lived to any considerable age, with the exception of one daughter who became a nun and thus escaped from the doctor's clutches. But without any such fatuous disrespect for a great name, I contend that W.G. was more proficient in slamming a long-hop through the covers than he was in shaking his thermometer at a bedside.

With imagination helpfully filling the gaps in memory I can visualise myself on the evening of that third and final day of my first of many Test Matches, poring over a match-card by now reduced to a state of begrimed disintegration. The names on that card were those of the experts who had gained top honours in a world of their own. Had it been revealed to me then (as in one of those informative New Testament dreams) that later in life I was to make the acquaintance of F. S. Jackson and Ranji, and to hobnob with Hugh Trumble and Clem Hill, my mother would have said, 'The excitement's been too much for him, Frank,' and would have busied herself mixing a sleeping-draught. But one thing about that night of 12 August 1896 I can most definitely affirm—I went to bed a dedicated, life-long cricket lover.

Since, as I have already mentioned, the present-day com-

KENNINGTON OVAL August 1896

ENGLAND

	1st inns.		2nd inns.	
W. G. Grace	c. Trott b. Giffen	24	b. Trumble	9
F. S. Jackson	c. McKibbin b. Trumble	45	b. Trumble	2
K. S. Ranjitsinhji	b. Giffen	8	st. Kelly b. McKibbin	11
R. Abel	c. & b. Trumble	26	c. Giffen b. Trumble	21
A. C. MacLaren	b. Trumble	20	b. Jones	6
T. Hayward	b. Trumble	0	c. Trott b. Trumble	13
E. G. Wynyard	c. Darling b. McKibbin	10	c. Kelly b. McKibbin	3
R. Peel	b. Trumble	0	b. Trumble	0
A. A. Lilley	c. Iredale b. Trumble	2	c. McKibbin b. Trumble	6
J. T. Hearne	b. McKibbin	8	b. McKibbin	1
T. Richardson	not out	1	not out	10
	Extras	1	Extras	2
	Total	145	Total	84

Bowling	O.	M.	R.	W.	O.	M.	R.	W.
Giffen	32	12	64	2	1	0	4	0
Trumble	40	10	59	6	25	9	30	6
McKibbin	9.3	0	21	2	20	8	35	3
Jones					3	0	13	1

AUSTRALIA

J. Darling	c. MacLaren b. Hearne	47	b. Hearne	0
F. A. Iredale	run out	30	c. Jackson b. Hearne	3
G. Giffen	b. Hearne	0	b. Hearne	1
G. H. S. Trott	b. Peel	5	c. sub b. Peel	3
S. E. Gregory	b. Hearne	1	c. Richardson b. Peel	6
C. Hill	run out	1	b. Peel	0
H. Donnan	b. Hearne	10	c. Hayward b. Peel	0
J. J. Kelly	not out	10	l.b.w. b. Peel	3
H. Trumble	b. Hearne	3	not out	7
E. Jones	c. MacLaren b. Peel	3	b. Peel	3
T. R. McKibbin	b. Hearne	0	c. Abel b. Hearne	16
	Extras	9	Extras	2
	Total	119	Total	44

Bowling	O.	M.	R.	W.	O.	M.	R.	W.
Peel	20	9	30	2	12	5	23	6
Hearne	26.1	10	41	6	13	8	19	4
Richardson	5	0	22	0	1	1	0	0
Hayward	2	0	17	0				

England won by 66 runs

7

mentators seemed to regard me as some spirit from the vasty deep of cricket history, I ought perhaps to have one more look at the names of that England side; names which now mean to the younger generation what 'my Hornby and my Barlow' mean to me. Bobby Abel was Surrey's diminutive, desperately consistent, opening batsman, who first played for England in 1888 when I was one year old. Tom Hayward was Abel's opening partner for Surrey. I was to see a lot of him subsequently— a tremendously long lot on one occasion (315 not out in a county game). E. G. Wynyard was an Old Carthusian Army man who had been enjoying a great season for Hampshire. Peel of Yorkshire vied with Briggs of Lancashire as the leading left-arm spin bowler of that time. Lilley, the Warwickshire wicketkeeper, like his opposite number, Kelly of Australia, was the accepted and permanent wicket-keeper for his country for the best part of twenty years. J. T. Hearne was England's best medium-slow right-arm-bowler then, and for some time to come. I remember him chiefly on account of his unique action. Just before delivery he held both arms out at full stretch horizontally and his right arm would come forward and propel the ball, without appearing to rise an inch above the shoulder. There have been bowlers since of whom the same may be said (Grimmett often used to bowl from somewhere round his right thigh) but I have never come across a bowler since Hearne who found it natural to adopt this rhythmic square-on method.

And then—Tom Richardson. Is it an old stager's obsession if I still cling to the conviction that Richardson was the greatest fast bowler that England has ever possessed? There have been faster speedmen no doubt: Tyson and Larwood were probably quicker than Richardson, while in the early years of the century there were three amateurs: W. M. Bradley, C. J. Kortright, W. Brearley, all of whom were very fast indeed. I wonder how many arguments used to take place in the pavilions and pubs of the past as to whether Kortright was speedier than Bradley, and what about Brearley if he really chose to let one go? Then there was W. B. Burns of Worcester. He used to be asked to open the bowling for just the first two or three overs, after which no human frame could be expected to expend such energy and to maintain such a phenomenal speed. If I was not afraid of appearing a cranky old wiseacre I might still confidently assert that W. B. Burns remains to this day the fastest of the lot.

In any case, at the time of that first Test Match of mine, Richardson was still recognised as England's fastest bowler; faster than Mold of Lancashire, who ruled himself out anyhow because he had once or twice been no-balled for throwing. Richardson's contemporary Australian rival was Ernest Jones, who was possibly a shade the quicker of the two. Jones, too, was alleged to be a thrower but he managed to get away with it. All I can say is that, whether he threw or not, he dismissed a good many batsmen in his time.

Neither Jones nor Richardson was called upon to play any great part in that spinner's match at the Oval. Richardson bowled six overs in the whole game and Jones only three. But at least I was given my first opportunity of gazing upon my hero. That tall figure, massive in chest and shoulders—the black moustache which seemed to constitute a special independent menace of its own (like that of my terrifying form-master, Mr Gulliver, at my prep-school)—I welcomed Richardson into the company of the other Titans of his time: Sandow, tearing three packs of cards in half with a turn of the wrist, Hackenschmidt, the Russian lion, and Madrali, the Terrible Turk, seeking to dislocate each other in the wrestling ring.

The records books give ample evidence of Tom Richardson's accuracy in line and length but his great distinction was his ability to maintain the line and length, without losing any speed, for such a prodigious spell. My estimate of him as our greatest-ever fast bowler may seem high-flown, but I'll swear that none has surpassed or even approached him in stamina.

I was to be compensated for seeing so little of Richardson in action at my initiation—and the term 'in action' is appropriate:

9

perfect rotation and high-speed delivery from the full arm's length above the six feet plus. In the course of the following few years I saw him once or twice at the Oval, with Lockwood, his Surrey fast-bowler partner, operating at the other end. Lockwood was to succeed Richardson as England's pace man. He had the most beautiful action I have ever seen—a springy little leap as he reached the crease, with his left arm extended towards the batsman and then a lovely flowing delivery of the ball with his right hand. I watched Yorkshire who, forced to follow on, were bowled out twice by Richardson and Lockwood on one Saturday afternoon. In the course of the Yorkshire procession, George Hirst on his way out passed Lord Hawke, the Yorkshire captain, on his way in and I remember the wry smile that Lord Hawke gave Hirst. Another of those little items which, for some reason, remain imbedded in one's cricket memories throughout the years.

However sceptical people may be about my estimate of Tom Richardson's bowling ability, one fact is universally recognised and unchallenged : he could and did drink a larger number of pints of beer on end than any known cricketer alive or dead. This alone is surely confirmation of my claims regarding his stamina.

And. A. C. MacLaren. The *and* is like that '*and*' which you see on theatre posters. It is at the foot of the cast but you are impressed as it carries the name of the leading support player printed in only slightly smaller capitals than those of the lead. He succeeded W.G. as England's captain and, although he never physically dominated the proceedings in the same way as the old man had, MacLaren did impose himself as the supreme General Officer in command of the Forces. He was of average height but high-shouldered and his whole personality was awesome; he even awed me as I watched him catching those high catches and I was glad he wasn't one of my school-masters, along with Mr Gulliver. I think that it was under MacLaren's captaincy that Test Matches against Australia began to be taken seriously as matters of national prestige. No longer any slapping on the back and, 'Well done : never mind, we'll drub you next time,' sort of thing. I cannot picture MacLaren patting any Australians on the back.

The names on that all-star cricket poster—W.G. at top, the leading star, with the list of chief supporting players, Hobbs, Trumper, Bradman and who you will—should still feature that *and* A. C. MacLaren at the foot. Why? There have been greater batsmen but at least he was among the great. To have made 424 in a single innings in a county match proves his superiority. Superiority—that was the whole substance of MacLaren's make-up. Superiority in his belief in himself, in his whole aspect, in his whole procedure.

Gentlemen and Players. The distinction was accepted in those days as the natural order of things. That the whole game should become a professional job within my middle lifetime, or middle-and-leg lifetime, was as inconceivable as men landing on the moon. Then and for many years later it was a recognised essential that every county should be captained by a Gentleman. And MacLaren was the Gentleman captain supreme, not only of the county but the country—the boss.

How good a boss he was of the England sides I can, of course, never know, but my observation of him on several occasions goes to confirm tradition that, however good a captain he was, he could be a pretty obnoxious one. He was said to have been unpopular with the Players, intimidating them and often being severely critical of them to their faces with the rest of the pro side looking on.

He was critical not only of Players but of fish. At the Hastings Festival a year or two later I was seated at the next table to him at an hotel breakfast. He took one taste of his herring and shouted across the room at the waiter : 'Come here, you. Take it away. It stinks.' I conjecture that at any moment of sudden displeasure his reactions were much the same on the cricket field as at the breakfast table.

Then why the '*And*'? Because, although he ranks among the very great as a batsman, MacLaren's countenance, rather like that of an eagle in sullen mood, glares from the far distance and challenges me to recall a personality more domineering.

I was back at the Oval with my father on 15 August 1899, but for that day only. I still showed on my thighs the bruises resulting from a term-time encounter in an inter-school match with a startling and horrendous prodigy of a boy bowler named J. N. Crawford. He must have been very nearly as fast then as he was when he bowled for England only six years later (medium-fast by first-class standards).

W.G. had, as I have said, given up Test cricket by 1899 but

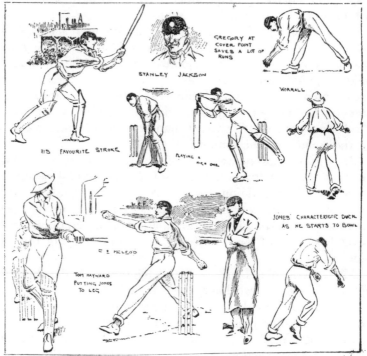

THE LAST TEST MATCH: ENGLAND'S FIRST INNINGS AT THE OVAL

there were plenty of compensations for me in the shape of some interesting newcomers from Australia : V. Trumper and M. A.

Noble. Lockwood had superseded Richardson as England's fast bowler and W. M. Bradley was also being given a fling. C. B. Fry and Rhodes had already established themselves.

My day there, the second day of the match, is still well remembered without being particularly memorable. England, batting first on the previous day, had already piled up a lot of runs, with Jackson and Hayward both making centuries in an opening partnership. Ranji had come and gone for 54 and Fry was not out 60 overnight. I watched him receive his first ball on the second morning. It was bowled (or thrown) at him by Ernest Jones, and Fry hit it into what looked to me to be the edge of eternity but it turned out that an Australian named Worrall was lingering there. Oh, what a stomach-sinking disappointment. C. B. Fry—after all I'd heard about him—out first ball.

England cantered comfortably along and were all out for 576. Australia proceeded to lay the foundations of the obvious draw, although Lockwood next day finished their innings off with 7 for 71, having bowled 40.3 overs and made them follow on. Trumper made only 6 when I was there. On the whole this was the least momentous of my first three Oval Test Matches, sandwiched between the magnetism of the first and the thrill of a lifetime which was awaiting me in 1902. But I would still like to recall the England side which I had watched in the field on that 1899 afternoon. In order of batting: F. S. Jackson, Hayward (T), K. S. Ranjitsinhji, C. B. Fry, A. C. MacLaren, C. K. Townsend, W. M. Bradley, Lockwood (W. H.), A. O. Jones, Lilley (A. A.), Rhodes (W). Townsend was a tall, lithe, Gloucestershire all-rounder in great form at the time. A. O. Jones was the captain of Nottinghamshire. He had a peculiar, flat stance with his left leg protruding from the batting crease. He was also a slow-leg-break right-arm bowler, though he seldom allowed himself much exercise in this department. Perhaps MacLaren gambled on the Jones type of bowling being a novelty to the Australians; anyhow, Jones was in operation quite early on and took their first two wickets including that of Trumper. So A. O. Jones made his mark and was taken on the next tour to Australia, by which time MacLaren seems to have dismissed him from much esteem, for Jones was given only one over to bowl in the course of five Test Matches.

Two

Jessop's Match

In August 1902 I was fifteen years old, a public schoolboy; licensed to find my own way to and from Kennington Oval, to occupy the stand seat booked for me for the full three days, to adjudge rather than to goggle at the proceedings in the middle and to overhear with a smirk of superior sagacity the unenlightened comments of my neighbours. My seat was in the third or fourth row from the front in the covered stand to the right of the pavilion nearest the gasometers, in what to a later generation of Ovalites was to be familiarly known as Sandham's Corner.

By the time they got to the Oval for the last Test of that tour the Australians had already won, or rather retained, the Ashes, but the score-books of the four previous Tests that year go to show that there was precious little to choose between the sides. The weather had played a great part in the undertakings. It enabled Rhodes to take 7 wickets for 17 and Hirst 3 for 15 in Australia's first innings (in the first Test at Edgbaston) which totalled 36, of which Trumper made exactly half, but England were left with no time in which to settle the matter when Australia followed on 340 behind.

The second Test at Lord's had been abandoned within an hour or so of its start. The Australians seem to have won the third match at Sheffield fair and square, thanks to a second innings century by Clem Hill in a low-scoring game. The fourth Test at Manchester was also a comparatively low-scoring affair, though Trumper and Jackson each obliged with a century. But this was the match which still claims a little niche of its own in the Wisden museum, recording as it does the tragedy of

F. W. Tate, father of Maurice Tate and last man in and out for England. Having scored four runs in the last innings, he was driven to remain weatherbound in the pavilion with only four more wanted for victory. As a result of this protracted and exasperating ordeal it was almost inevitable that Australia should snatch the three-run win.

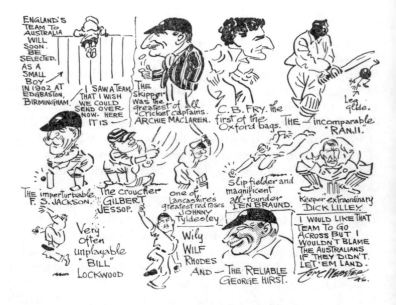

But Ashes be blowed, there was no cheerless feeling of anti-climax in my mind as I eagerly awaited the start of that Oval match on the morning of 11 August 1902. We were better than they were and, to get thoroughly revenged on them in this final Test, would jolly well show them so. From the abnormal display of general rejoicing which greeted the outcome, it would appear that a great many other people shared this view, though they could not, of course, attain my astute, teenage perspicuity.

Five of the Australians from my 1896 team were still on view : J. Darling (now captain), S. E. Gregory, Hill, Trumble and Kelly. Meanwhile Trumper had arrived not merely to strengthen the side but to create a challenge of his own, and Noble was busy establishing himself as Australia's greatest ever all-rounder. The massive figure of W. W. Armstrong, together with R. A. Duff (Trumper's opening partner), A. Hopkins and J. V. Saunders were all new to me. Saunders had taken over from E. Jones, who had now ceased to throw for his country. I bore a private grudge against Saunders, for it had been he who had skittled the unfortunate Tate on the latter's belated return to the wicket in the previous Test. Saunders was a medium-pace left-arm bowler, rather like Alan Davidson of more recent times; though he wasn't as fast as Davidson, nor, I imagine, as good a bowler. Few were.

Neither Ranji nor Fry appeared for England. This was hardly surprising. They had each had four innings in the series; Ranji's contributions having been 13, 0, 2 and 4 and Fry's 0, 0, 1 and 4. L. C. H. Palairet, a Somerset amateur, who was regarded as one of England's most stylish batsmen, was being given his second chance as an opener and J. T. Tyldesley, the Lancashire pro, had earned himself a permanent place in the side with an innings of 138 in the first of these five Tests. L. C. Braund, of Somerset, was an all-rounder (medium-slow right-arm bowler) who had also held his place on merit in the five games. These, along with G. L. Jessop, who had been in and out of the England side in the 1899 Australian tour and in Australia since then, were my newcomers this time.

As I sit once again for those three days in Sandham's Corner (Andy Sandham was just twelve years old at the time and might have been there too—but, alas, wasn't, he tells me) my eye lights upon a strange figure. Is it possible that these words may be read by some fellow-nonagenarian who recalls Craig, the 'Surrey Poet'? A tall, grey, hatless mountebank, he must somehow have prevailed upon the local cricket authorities to grant him licence to tour the boundaries of the Oval playing area, selling at a penny a sheet the ill-copper-plated samples of his doggerel. He was for years an unchallenged, taken-for-granted presence during all first-class matches on his home ground. At one time I possessed a Craig tribute to Robert Abel and can still memorise the concluding lines:

Harry Wood has a story I've oft heard him tell,
That the sparrows themselves know when Bobby does well:
They take a front seat 'mid the cricketing throng
And when Bob gets his cent'ry they burst into song.
(Harry Wood was the Surrey wicket-keeper.)

Now, after almost eighty years, Jessop's Match still seems to retain a special sort of fabulous and glamorous reputation of its own. When I mentioned it in that commentators' eyrie the immediate response was, 'That match—Jessop's match—you saw that?' Primed with John Arlott's Moët I told them a bit about it. But what bit? Simply the finish and some of the details of the never-to-be-forgotten last day's play leading up to that finish. And now that I come to write about it I find myself faced with the fact that the first two days' play contained some incidents which tickle the memory but few to haunt it.

I am glad now that I watched Trumper starting off the match with a characteristic 42, for it was the only time I ever saw Trumper make double figures. But the latter-end of the first day's play produced in me a good deal of lingering resentment and muffled snorting as Trumble persisted in a long and stubborn tail-ender's innings of 64 not out ('pottering about' in my view) and, along with Hopkins and Kelly, put on about 150 for the eighth and ninth wickets. The second morning belonged to Trumble too, as bowler this time, unchanged throughout England's first knock and taking 8 for 65. As a result England were left 141 behind, which was all pretty depressing, but we had a great stroke of luck when Australia batted again. Trumper had only made two when he went for a quick run, stumbled, fell flat halfway down the pitch and was run out. Then Lockwood put in a great spell of bowling and Australia were all out soon after the start of the third morning for 121 (Lockwood 5 for 45). So the second day was a great deal more

18

eventful than the tedious first and I am sure I watched every ball with those hopes and fears which only the cricket lover can appreciate. But it is no good pretending that I can still give an eye-witness account of all that happened. Some of those for-no-particular-reason incidents survive. I remember one immaculate cover-drive of Palairet's better than I remember any individual cover-drive of Hammond's or Hutton's. Above all, two first-slip catches by MacLaren. They were not difficult catches; they came straight into his hands. It was the manner with which he accepted them. He took the ball and tossed it, not over his head to recatch it, but away into outer space with a flick of the wrist in the most disdainful fashion. 'Take it away: it stinks.' Oh, yes, yes; the name of A. C. MacLaren will always honour that *'and'*— at any rate on *my* cricket poster.

Trumble and Lockwood must in turn have demonstrated that, ever since the first day, the wicket had got worse and worse. After England's first innings total of 183 and Australia's second innings total of 121, how could we possibly be expected to make 263 to win? We couldn't, of course, but the impossibility needn't have been rubbed in to me so cruelly. That hateful Saunders immediately came sailing in at the Vauxhall end, slinging destruction. MacLaren b. Saunders 2, Palairet b. Saunders 6, Tyldesley b. Saunders 0, Hayward c. Kelly b. Saunders 7. Jackson, at number five, was not out at lunchtime. Braund had joined him, but only for a very short time (c. Kelly b. Trumble 2).

During the lunch interval I noticed quite a number of disgruntled elderly members gathering up their belongings in the pavilion and departing home, unable to face the indignity of witnessing England's abasement. And I wonder what MacLaren had to say about what was served up to him for his mid-day meal.

So then—Braund out but with Jackson still there and appearing remarkably unruffled. And in came Jessop.

Jessop was a favourite subject for Craig's contemporary rivals as cricket poets. I recall two pleasing lines from an unidentified bard:

> At one end stocky Jessop crouched,
> The human catapult—

Crouched was an obvious description: 'the croucher' was a familiar nickname for Jessop owing to his stance at the wicket. 'Stocky' was descriptive of him too, though I think 'jaunty' would be nearer the mark. I knew, of course, all about his

Jessop hits Trumble on to the Pavilion for the second
time in one over.

reputation as the biggest hitter in the game, but he had disappointed us in England's first innings (b. Trumble 13). Oh, well—perhaps he might treat us to a good slog or two before the inevitable and dismal defeat.

Again I must stick to my genuine and lasting recollections and impressions. It is obviously impossible to recall that Jessop innings in detail but there are certain features of it, and of its effect upon the crowd, that remain as clearly in my mind as though it all happened yesterday. To begin with, I was struck by Jessop's undaunted, almost it seemed heedless, approach— no 'desperate situation' about it. Jaunty. He was his own aggressive self from the start. Before long he took the triumphant Saunders in hand, to my especial delight, and hit him for two fours off successive balls to the long-on boundary. Darling immediately posted two fielders out there but Jessop ignored them and hit Saunders' next two deliveries between them or round them or through them as well. However despondent the crowd must have been during the morning, Jessop aroused them now to a state of wild exhilaration and Jackson must have been scoring steadily on his own. But I confess that the only thing I can remember about Jackson's invaluable innings is his getting caught and bowled by Trumble when he had made 49 and Jackson's exasperated thump with his bat on his pad as he turned to go.

Oh, damn and blast. Any faint gleam of hope of our getting those 263 runs vanished with Jackson into the pavilion. But the Australians had still another Yorkshireman to deal with. Confidence was the last thing that Jessop seemed to require but, had he needed it, George Hirst was the man to supply it— sturdy, defiant and the best all-rounder in the country in his day. (No one else had ever taken 200 wickets and made 2,000 runs in one season and they never will.) Sure enough, Hirst settled down while Jessop continued as before. Trumble was still on at the pavilion end. Still on? He was never off throughout the whole of England's two innings. Jessop hit him for six on to a canvas awning above part of the members' enclosure.

The ball came back only to land on almost exactly the same spot immediately afterwards.

On they went, Hirst unmoveable, Jessop irrepressible. Presently the roars of the crowd subsided and gave way to an awesome, aspiring hush. They had roared Jessop to the verge of his century.

How well all cricket lovers know that tremulous moment and, goodness me, how often have I experienced it myself, but never, never in my whole life has it meant to me what it meant then.

Hush. Jessop crouched. The bowler started his run. It was just as well for me that my heart was only fifteen years old. The bowler bowled. Bang. Uproar.

The conventional Londoner wore a hat in those days and the conventional hat he wore was a straw boater. As Jessop made that stroke dozens of straw boaters were sent sailing from the crowd like boomerangs. Unlike boomerangs they failed to return to the owners, but who cared?

Like all cricket devotees I have many, many times shared with all around me that infectious, 'breathless hush' tension as a batsman, however well-set, however self-possessed, has to face up to the obligation of scoring that hundredth run. He brings it off and, amid the general enthusiasm, one feels a spasm of pleasurable secret relief and a glow of fraternal satisfaction in the case of a batsman one is particularly fond of. I know I was young and almost foolishly impressionable at the time but I have always treasured and still treasure that century of Jessop's above and apart from all the rest.

The frenzy gradually subsided; boaters were or were not recovered; the crowd settled down. England still had a long way to go; but so long as Jessop and Hirst were there . . . Then, oh, no, Jessop mistimed a hook-shot and was caught at fine leg. What a tragedy. But that seemed to settle it; that stupendous effort of 104 was sacrificed. We couldn't hope to win now, could we? Hirst was still battling away and scoring steadily but Lockwood didn't last long. Lilley did though.

Beyond all expectation Lilley stuck there with Hirst. The score crept up—230, 240—the whole Oval became almost as intent and intimidated as I was, hesitating to applaud too loudly for fear of inciting Hirst and Lilley to rashness.

Lilley got caught for 16 when the total had reached 248. Fifteen wanted and Rhodes came in to join his fellow Yorkshireman for a last-wicket partnership which was to become a sort of historic addendum to Jessop's hundred: though the legend that Hirst greeted Rhodes with the pronouncement: 'We'll get 'em in singles,' was later refuted by Rhodes himself. They got 'em steadily, a single here a couple there, until they'd levelled up the match at 262.

That is the moment—or rather the marathon minute—which remains clearest of all in my memory. Duff was fielding at deep long-on to Trumble, who was bowling, as ever, from the pavilion end. An Australian from his seat in the stand a few rows behind me shouted, 'Never mind, Duff; you've won the Ashes.' I saw Duff turn his head with a quick resigned grin and return at once to attention. He of all the Australians in the field was required to be at attention. Trumble, as crafty a bowler as ever existed, presented Rhodes with a slow half-volley on the leg stump. How could any human batsman resist such a heaven-sent gift? 'Hurrah, here it is and here it goes'—wallop. And the ball would sail high into the outfield and, well within the range of possibility, into the safe hands of Duff. Not Rhodes. Not Yorkshire. Rhodes tapped the ball gently past square leg, ran the safe single and the match was won.

When by some means long forgotten I managed to arrive back home that evening, there was my father waiting to welcome me in the open doorway, his arms outstretched in mutual rejoicing. I felt a bit of a hero at having actually been there on Jessop's Day. I still do.

In the world of sport of those days cricket was held in a privileged regard of its own. During the summer seasons cricket was a logical, routine opening topic of conversation at City luncheons, West End clubs and barbers' shops. It was only to be expected that England's victory caused a sudden tidal wave of public jubilation. In sentiment if not in actual demonstration it was a modest echo of the recent unprecedented exultations of Mafeking Night. This almost miraculous restoration of our prestige was hailed with panegyrics which overlooked the fact that the prestige had been in dire and ignominious need of restoration. Who cared about the Ashes now? Boaters in the air.

The newspaper versifiers had the time of their lives:

> A Croucher at the wicket took his stand
> And thrashed the Cornstalk trundlers to the ropes.

Two or three nights after the great event I was taken to Daly's Theatre, which was on the site of Warner's Theatre in Leicester Square, to see *A Country Girl*. This was a musical comedy produced on lines familiar to habitués of Daly's. One of the acclaimed contributions to these Daly's shows was the 'topical song', delivered by a popular and portly vocalist named Rutland Barrington, with lyrics introduced to suit the occasion. His character was 'The Rajah of Bhong' and the title of his topical song was, 'Peace, peace . . . In the beautiful valley of Bhong.' On this night he obliged with the following final encore:

> There's a game that we play on a bright summer's day
> With a bat and a ball and a wicket,
> And we always had thought when we joined in the sport
> That we really were playing at cricket;
> But Australians came just to give us a game
> And, although it is painful to say it,
> They were teaching us fast we were things of the past
> And we really don't know how to play it.
> *Chorus*
> Peace—two innings apiece
> And none of them last very long:
> Only Jackson and Mac could withstand the attack
> Of our friends from the Valley of Bhong.

Repeat chorus
Peace—two innings apiece
And none of them last very long,
Until Jessop and Hirst brought old England in first—

If Barrington sang a last line no one heard it. The whole audience burst into a roar; many of the male customers rose spontaneously to their feet. It was just one illustration of the almost hysterical general jubilation at the result of Jessop's Match.

My public-school career was distinguished for its remarkable lack of distinction. There were only two subjects in which I was exceptionally well-informed and they didn't get me anywhere. I could have rattled off the name of the show that was on at any London theatre at the time, along with the respective author, composer and every advertised member of the cast. And I had watched or knew all about every established or up-and-coming player in first-class county cricket. If some fantastic, Alice-in-Wonderland curriculum had been in vogue at Charterhouse I might well have been head of the school.

As it was, my cricket-watching opportunities became sadly restricted from 1904 onwards and for a long time ahead. On leaving Charterhouse I was sent to the City, a fate reserved for any school numbskull who had failed to qualify for the 'Varsity or for a prospect in one of the professions. Everybody worked until one o'clock on Saturdays then, and county matches ended their three days on the Saturday, so a dash to the Oval for the expiring four hours of a game was seldom worthwhile. Moreover my obvious distaste for commerce proved stronger even than my attachment to cricket and the theatre. I volunteered to go into exile on the staff of the company's branch in Singapore, a suggestion readily accepted by the board of directors.

After all, I could still keep up my interest in cricket; but if I were going to be permanently stuck in the City with no time off to watch it, what could be more tantalising and tiresome?

KENNINGTON OVAL August 1902

AUSTRALIA

	1st inns.		2nd inns.	
V. Trumper	b. Hirst	42	run out	2
R. A. Duff	c. Lilley b. Hirst	23	b. Lockwood	0
C. Hill	b. Hirst	11	c. MacLaren b. Hirst	34
J. Darling	c. Lilley b. Hirst	3	c. MacLaren b. Lockwood	15
M. A. Noble	c. & b. Jackson	52	b. Braund	13
S. E. Gregory	b. Hirst	23	b. Braund	9
W. W. Armstrong	b. Jackson	17	b. Lockwood	21
A. Hopkins	c. MacLaren b. Lockwood	40	c. Lilley b. Lockwood	3
H. Trumble	not out	64	not out	7
J. J. Kelly	c. Rhodes b. Braund	39	l.b.w. b. Lockwood	0
J. V. Saunders	l.b.w. b. Braund	0	c. Tyldesley b. Rhodes	2
	Extras	10	Extras	9
	Total	324	Total	121

Bowling	O.	M.	R.	W.	O.	M.	R.	W.
Rhodes	28	9	46	0	22	7	38	1
Hirst	29	5	77	5	5	1	7	1
Braund	16.5	5	29	2	9	1	15	2
Jackson	20	4	66	2	—	—	—	—
Jessop	6	2	11	0	—	—	—	—
Lockwood	24	2	85	1	20	6	45	5

ENGLAND

	1st inns.		2nd inns.	
A. C. MacLaren	c. Armstrong b. Trumble	10	b. Saunders	2
L. C. H. Palairet	b. Trumble	20	b. Saunders	6
J. T. Tyldesley	b. Trumble	33	b. Saunders	0
T. Hayward	b. Trumble	0	c. Kelly b. Saunders	7
F. S. Jackson	c. Armstrong b. Saunders	2	c. & b. Trumble	49
L. C. Braund	c. Hill b. Trumble	22	c. Kelly b. Trumble	2
G. L. Jessop	b. Trumble	13	c. Noble b. Armstrong	104
G. H. Hirst	c. & b. Trumble	43	not out	58
W. H. Lockwood	c. Noble b. Saunders	25	l.b.w. b. Trumble	2
A. A. Lilley	c. Trumper b. Trumble	0	c. Darling b. Trumble	16
W. Rhodes	not out	0	not out	6
	Extras	15	Extras	11
	Total	183	Total	263

Bowling	O.	M.	R.	W.	O.	M.	R.	W.
Trumble	31	13	65	8	33.5	4	108	4
Saunders	23	7	79	2	24	3	105	4
Noble	7	3	24	0	5	0	11	0
Armstrong	—	—	—	—	4	0	28	1

England won by 1 wicket

In those schoolboy years from 1896 to 1904 I had enjoyed the experience of having seen them all, all the greatest and some of the greatest at their greatest—the Old Man himself, Ranji, Jackson, Richardson, Lockwood, Hirst, Jessop, Rhodes, Trumper, Clem Hill, Trumble—oh, and now I must remember to include those two great wicket-keepers who functioned as regularly as clockwork for their two countries for all those and several other years, Lilley and Kelly. Apart from a vague idea of what they looked like, I do not recall any of their particular moments behind the stumps, which is surely proof of what efficient wicket-keepers they must have been. No doubt in those days the limitations set for themselves by bowlers made wicket-keeping a far less erratic job. Richardsons and Joneses did not call upon their keepers to perform gymnastics and somersaults which we associate nowadays with Knott, Marsh and Murray.

During those summer holidays from school I had also seen other prominent players most of whom had played for England at one time or another. There was the rather quaint and miniature W. G. Quaife of Warwickshire (he was shorter even than Bobby Abel). He did not appear to deny or disprove the unenviable reputation of being the slowest scoring batsman in the game, or in the cricketing term of the time 'the champion poke'. There were William and John Gunn of Nottinghamshire (George Gunn was to come later and thank goodness he did). William Gunn specialised in the genuine late cut, a stroke which one seldom sees today; just once or twice perhaps in an innings from a well-set West Indian. William Gunn perfected and employed it in a way which was unforgettable. There was a splendid Middlesex amateur left-hander named F. G. J. Ford, who had toured for England in Australia in 1895. He stood very upright and had as cracking a clean straight drive through the bowler's half-circle as anyone I can think of. I saw him cruelly knocked out of first-class cricket at that same Hastings Festival when MacLaren expressed dislike for his herring. The ball was not aimed at Ford's head—no one had to wear these revolting safety headgears against bowlers of Richardson's methods and principles—but it struck another portion of the anatomy severely enough to bring an end to the career of one of the most stylish and delightful batsmen of his or any other age. And, apart from Ford, I don't suppose there was anyone on the ground who was sorrier than Richardson or more disappointed than I was.

I only wish that there were more cricket lovers still surviving to share my pleasure in looking back and visualising, as I do, some of those individuals whom I used to find specially appealing; who could again sit beside me and watch D. L. A. Jephson of Surrey, sending down his underhand lobs and being treated with the utmost suspicion by normally aggressive batsmen. (I never saw Jessop tackle him : I wish I had.) Others, forgotten now, made this special appeal to me so greatly then that I feel it a duty to myself to mention them—Brockwell, Wainwright of Yorkshire, and J. R. Mason of Kent; all three consistent all-rounders, they let me down rather sadly on their respective tours to Australia. All through my life certain cricketers, sometimes only moderate performers, have attracted my particular interest and my keenness for their success. Perhaps this is the case with all lovers of the game.

I know what my primary reason was for my anxious loyalty to J. R. Mason. He had been at my prep school—a few years before I had arrived there, of course. But another member of the Kent County side, E. W. Dillon, had actually been captain of the school during my first term. So one morning, soon after I had been granted licence to go about alone, I set eagerly forth for Catford, where Kent were due to begin a county match against Yorkshire. Arriving early, as eager small boys do, I observed the Yorkshire captain, Lord Hawke, inspecting the pitch with his fast bowler, Haigh. Still obeying the natural instincts of the eager small boy on a cricket ground, I edged in to overhear the consultation. The Catford groundsman can only very rarely have been called upon to prepare a first-class wicket and his lordship took a somewhat critical view of his efforts. I heard him tell Haigh, 'I think you might be able to do something with this,' and Haigh agreed with deferential readiness. Lord Hawke won the toss and put Kent in. Kent were all out for about twopence and Haigh took eight wickets. I was sorry for Kent but Mason and Dillon each made a few and I felt an irresistible satisfaction at having participated in their downfall. Just another example of how clearly and durably those cricket memories of my boyhood entered into my soul.

This delectable twelve-year period of boyhood cricket watching ended in 1904. This was just at the time when cricket itself was emerging from its youth into the full bloom of manhood. Its development was rapid. W. L. Murdoch, who was still playing first-class cricket in 1904, when he made 140 on one occasion, had figured in the second Test Match ever played since the game began in Melbourne 1877. He and his contemporaries, playing under regulations long superseded and in conditions now considered primitive (and so they often were), not only sustained the game in its early years but pioneered it into strenuous and stimulating conflict. Their performances, though not in some cases their capabilities, have long been exceeded to an extent which has relegated them to obscurity. Plenty of historic contests, innumerable historic achievements have been recorded since their last innings ended all those years ago. But thank goodness I was granted the privilege of watching those splendid old forefathers paving the way. That capacious frame with the beard and the striped cap and the left toe cocked and the bat held six inches from the crease still remains a figure apart.

Three

Out There

Whenever, throughout the English cricket season, a batch of newspapers found their way from home to Singapore, three weeks ante-dated, my commercial activities in Raffles Square (miskeeping pineapple ledgers and making bad debts with Chinese grocers) were suspended for the day. I returned to London in 1908 to more congenial employment, but employment which still entailed this same old office routine of Saturday afternoons off only. I have set out to deal with matches and players that I saw for myself and, through the years from 1908 to the outbreak of war in 1914, my opportunities were very limited, though I took them when I could at odd times. But at such odd times, and for however briefly, I was able to inspect some of those who had staked a claim as England players; established indeed in the case of Hobbs and Woolley. But there were others, newcomers to me, such as George Gunn, J. W. Hearne, J. W. H. T. Douglas, F. R. Foster and J. N. Crawford, though I had previously not only seen but felt the effects of the latter. This, too, was the period during which S. F. Barnes soared to fame. Alas, I never saw him bowl. I went to the Oval on one Bank Holiday on purpose to do so, only to discover that he was laid up and couldn't perform. There was no adequate understudy whose name could appear on the slip in *that* programme. I have watched in turn all the English bowlers who have been heralded as the best of their time; but I feel pretty sure that I was deprived of watching the best of the whole bunch.

Of the top players during those years two only, Hobbs and Phil Mead, were to figure in the fulfilment of a day-dream. In

Gilbert Jessop, whose historic innings of 104 won the 1902 Oval test match against Australia for England, watched by an excited Ben Travers

Tom Richardson whom Ben considered '. . . the greatest fast bowler that England has ever possessed'

. C. Maclaren: '. . . the gentle-
an captain supreme . . . the
boss'

F. S. Jackson: '. . . remarkably
unruffled'

Bobby Abel: 'Surrey's diminutive, desperately consistent, opening
batsman'

'Plum' Warner: '. . . deserved a knighthood for his services to cricket'

D. R. Jardine: '. . . a stiff-necke high-nosed type'

J. M. Gregory, the great Australian fast bowler

Larwood: 'terrific pace'

The 'Kippax Incident' at Sydney, December 1928. The photo shows clearly that Kippax was indeed bowled

Ben with the 1930 Australian Team. *Back row, from left to right:* Don Bradman, Alec Hurwood, Percy Hornibrook, Ted a' Beckett, Tim Wall, (unknown, not a player), Clarrie Grimmett, Charlie Walker, Bill Ponsford; *Front row:* Stan McCabe, Alan Kippax, Ben, Vic Richardson, Arthur Mailey (accompanying team as journalist)

Jack Hobbs. Ben saw his debut for Surrey against The Gentlemen of England in 1905 and 'watched him play a delightful innings of 88'

Bradman '. . . must rank as the greatest slaughterer of bowling on record'

Percy Chapman: '. . . in his time there was no more flamboyant middle order attacking batsman'

Patsy Hendren: '. . . an infectious optimistic outlook'

George Gunn: '. . . what a character'

Alan Davidson: 'I have never seen an open spell so shattering'

Alan Kippax – gave Ben 'mo[re] pleasure to watch than any bat[s]man I have ever seen'

the early days of my Singapore sojourn I had read and re-read and re-read until I knew it in my head from cover to cover, a book called *How We Recovered the Ashes* by P. F. Warner, who had captained the England tour of Australia in 1903–4. And I had made a vow that one day, somehow, sooner or later, I would go and watch a series of Test Matches in that country. Warner's recapitulation of R. E. Foster's 287 in his first Test innings and of the baffling effects of B. J. T. Bosanquet's conjuring tricks on the opposing side became long-past history. The years went by. I was still denied the chance of watching more than a day's cricket here and there but my enthusiasm never wavered. The vow still held.

I daresay it lingered and occasionally cropped up in my mind during my four years as an air pilot in the 1914–18 War—one of those never-to-be-realised, almost ludicrous, ambitions of the past. I married in 1916 and after the war, having, like so many others, to find a new job for myself, I took to writing. We emigrated to Somerset, so at least I was free to watch first-class cricket again. But I was very conscientious and kept busy and yielded only to the temptation of some irresistible allurement at Taunton. Meanwhile I prospered as a playwright steadily and solidly and, like some old tree which had withered away over twenty years but had never quite died and which now suddenly burst into bloom, my long-treasured hope was fulfilled.

One morning in the autumn of 1928 my wife and I left Tilbury Dock in an Orient liner bound for Australia with England's cricket team on board. I met 'Plum' Warner only once and that was only for a few minutes in the Long Room in Lord's pavilion when he was far gone in years and I was gone a pretty long way myself. In the Lord's library on the same day I had been one of a small audience listening to C. B. Fry recounting his 'Varsity days when he used to take a standing jump from floor to mantelpiece and he offered to repeat the performance for our benefit. Interested as I was to enjoy this brief encounter with the greatest all-round athlete of my time, it gave me an even greater kick to meet 'Plum'. After all, it was he who had been solely responsible for all the pleasure I had got out of that trip to Australia in 1928–9 and the years following.

I had been at Lord's on the day when some of his county side had carried him on their shoulders into the pavilion on the final day of his Middlesex captaincy when Middlesex had just defeated Surrey to win the championship. If anyone ever deserved a knighthood for services to Cricket it was Sir Pelham. Not that he was ever to be rated as one of cricket's outstanding all-star performers; but in his capacity as impresario and producer, or, as he himself would have preferred to be regarded, the long-serving Archbishop of the game, nobody can ever be compared with him.

When I first went to Australia with that 1928 England side, the state of English cricket was that of someone making a sudden and complete recovery from a long illness and bursting into health and vigour. Since the war there had been twenty Test Matches played, of which England had won two (the fourteenth and the twentieth) and Australia twelve. We had suffered at the hands of a fresh batch of Australians, such as Macartney, Ryder, Bardsley, Ponsford and, above all, that devastating trio of bowlers, J. M. Gregory, E. A. McDonald and Arthur Mailey. But in 1928 all of them except Gregory had completed their course. The Australian selectors had some pretty wide gaps to fill, though they were already keeping two potential world-beaters, Archie Jackson and that fabulous boy from Bowral, D. G. Bradman, up their sleeve. With England it had been just the other way about. At last, and about time too, we had landed a bunch of players to supersede and out-shine the hotchpotch of excellent but mostly insecure representatives of the post-war era. On that liner with me was one of the best England sides on record—the best of all for my money.

Dear, dear, how old I am. To think that this all happened over fifty years ago and that some of the names in that team may ring only a faint tinkle in the ears of so many devotees today. Yet some of those listed names must surely endure for ever. Here they are:

A. P. F. Chapman (captain)
J. C. ('Farmer') White (vice-captain)
D. R. Jardine
J. B. Hobbs
H. Sutcliffe
W. R. Hammond
E. ('Patsy') Hendren
E. Tyldesley
M. Leyland
H. Larwood
M. W. Tate
G. Duckworth
G. Geary
L. Ames
A. P. ('Tich') Freeman
S. Staples
C. P. Mead

Sam Staples was taken ill early on in the tour and returned to England. He wasn't replaced. Leslie Ames was the understudy wicket-keeper to George Duckworth and did not figure in any of the Tests. My word, how largely he was to figure in many of the subsequent ones. 'Tich' Freeman was not called upon for the Tests either. I was in the England dressing-room at Brisbane when the side for the first Test was announced. 'Tich' held aloft his cricket-bag and shouted, 'Does anybody want to buy a nice cricketer's outfit?'

No one in England could understand why Frank Woolley had been left out of the side. He was still going as strong as ever and, in fact, played again in Tests against Australia in 1930 and 1934. Ernest Tyldesley, who had a very good season for Lancashire, was a fair enough candidate. Phil Mead had been plodding along down the years without ever showing his stumps to the bowler and refusing to be dislodged, but that he should have ousted Woolley raised a hell of a controversy. As it turned out Woolley wasn't wanted, but that only went to show how strong an all-round side it was.

I had watched seven of them playing in the Oval Test two years before. This was the match made memorable by a final and crowning effort on the part of Rhodes, recalled to the actual scene on which I had seen him pat that winning run no less than twenty-four years before. There cannot be many still alive, besides myself, who saw Rhodes put the finishing touch, or pat, to the proceedings on that delirious occasion in 1902; but there must surely be many who were with me to watch him in action for the last time in 1926. Anybody who saw Rhodes bowl will still be able to picture those three deliberate walking steps to the crease, the left forearm bent back to the left shoulder before rolling forward and over; the ball delivered with complete control, complete subtlety. In that last match of his, he and Larwood—a murderously contrasted couple—put paid to the Australians in the fourth innings. Once more I may appear to be a biased old-timer; but it is not merely my opinion, it is my definite knowledge that of all the immensely gifted left-arm slow bowlers Wisden can muster—Peel, Briggs, Blythe, Charlie Parker, Woolley, J. C. White, Verity, Underwood—there has never been one greater than Wilfred Rhodes.

But if this classic comeback of Rhodes rather stole the show, this 1926 Oval match was a very eventful and remarkable one in many respects. It retains a special little compartment of its own in my overworked but reliable brain-box. To begin with, when Hobbs and Sutcliffe appeared to have settled in nicely on the first morning, Arthur Mailey, taking over at the Pavilion end, astonished and clean bowled Hobbs with a slow full-toss. Sutcliffe continued unperturbed as usual and Percy Chapman banged up a carefree 49 but England totalled only 280. We managed to get rid of Australia for 302 but no sooner had we done so than a heavy overnight rainstorm flooded the pitch, and Hobbs and Sutcliffe had to engage in a long and fierce second innings opening on a beast of a drying wicket.

34

It is sad to think that now, with the first threatening cloud coming up, groundstaffs doubling out to the middle lugging acres of tarpaulin, no modern spectator can ever enjoy the tremulous fascination of cricket at its most enthralling—that of watching brilliant defensive batmanship against skilful spin bowling on a sticky wicket. The tension of those first two hours, while Hobbs and Sutcliffe clung on and stuck it out and saw it through, was almost unbearable. They survived the ordeal and both went on to make their centuries. They did more for me than to give me some of the most mesmeric, intimidating hours I had ever spent on a cricket ground. They had booked my passage to Australia.

I didn't set out on that voyage with any intention of getting to know the members of the England team. So far as I can remember, the only occasion I did so was when, during a day ashore at Naples, my wife and I coincided with Percy Chapman and his wife, Beat, the sister of T. C. Lowry, who, with Burt Sutcliffe and Martin Donnelly, played a leading part in putting New Zealand on the cricket map. In any case, my wife had planned to go only as far as what was then Colombo before returning to spend Christmas with our children. I stayed with her for a fortnight in Ceylon (now Sri Lanka) and then went ahead to Australia on my own. On this latter voyage I had the luck to discover C. G. Macartney as a fellow passenger. Charlie Macartney was nicknamed 'The Governor General', I don't know why, unless it was for his value to the Australian Test teams, but his name will always remain high on their roll of honour. It is chiefly renowned in this country for his having scored a century before lunch in one of the Tests here in 1926. He was a most amiable character who would, as will be seen, go out of his way to be helpful and considerate, but an altogether different personality when it came to preparing for battle in a Test. Arthur Mailey was to describe to me later how he used to watch Charlie Macartney, due to go in first wicket down, sitting, padded up on a pavilion balcony, his chin resting on the top of his bat handle, glaring out at what was going on and muttering aloud threatenings and slaughter : 'Come on; let me get at 'em.'

When we disembarked at Fremantle, the England team was due to perform shortly afterwards in Sydney, which was Macartney's home city. He and I put in a day at Melbourne on the way and he took me to the offices of the Victorian Cricket Association and introduced me to the Secretary, none other than the now venerable Hugh Trumble. The Hugh Trumble who, thirty-two years before, I had seen bowling to W. G. Grace—successfully too (Grace b. Trumble 9 in his second innings). The Trumble I had watched, twenty-four years before, with all a small schoolboy's vengeful glee, being carted by Jessop for two successive sixes. He was the most gentle and gracious old fellow and offered to do anything he could to help me to enjoy my visit. Presently into his room came another Australian cricket celebrity—not quite so gentle and gracious—Warwick Armstrong. Before I had seen a ball bowled in their country, I found myself in the company of three of the top-rankers in Australian cricket history at that time. A surprising and pleasing start to my sojourn. Its sole object had been that I might follow the progress of the England team from a respectful distance without any expectation of being welcomed into the inner ring.

But even more surprising and pleasing was what happened when I got to Sydney. I booked in at the English boys' hotel and was immediately received with open arms by Percy Chapman and borne into their midst. Right away I became not merely a modest camp-follower but a taken-for-granted member of the party.

Why? In those days, long before transport to Australia by air, it was an almost unheard-of thing for anybody to be so fanatical as to undertake the long and expensive tour simply to watch cricket. I think that, almost without knowing it, they felt an instinctive gratitude to me because they were the cricketers I was doing it for. The Australians, too, when I got to know them, appreciated my enterprise, regarding me as an admirably discriminating crank. Some of their past-masters, such as Clem Hill and Monty Noble, were particularly cordial. Noble had forestalled Archbishop Warner in his own country and was by then the self-appointed and acknowledged pontifex of Australian cricket. In this capacity Noble took it upon himself to organise and perform a special ceremony later in the tour. On one of the days of the third Test at Melbourne, which happened to be Jack Hobbs' birthday, Noble insisted that Hobbs should accompany him on a walking tour round the ground during the luncheon interval. What Jack Hobbs had to say about this I never knew and I don't think that Noble was motivated by anything beyond his profound admiration for Jack, combined with a genuine lifetime dedication to cricket nearer this side of idolatry than I have ever known in anybody. For many years now there has been on Sydney ground a stand erected and named The Noble Stand. I sat in it when I paid a visit to Australia in 1963 (when T. E. Dexter's touring side were playing Australia), alongside a Sydney lady enthusiast who devoured a large plateful of curry from her lap and kept shouting, 'Good on yer, Lawry,' between mouthfuls.

On my first visit to the Sydney ground in 1928 (it was the opening morning of our game against New South Wales), I was given a complimentary seat in the members' stand, which was, of course, an exclusively male establishment. In those days the Australians used to segregate the sexes even on their racecourses; I don't know whether they still do. But on the immediate right of the members' stand there was another large open stand which accommodated the more privileged of Sydney's female society, which seemed a pretty good idea to me (and, as will be seen later, to Wally Hammond). It enabled one to feast the eyes on a choice selection of, I think, the best-looking women in the world (Ireland a close second) without having to listen to their conversation. But they were keen followers of the game and at any exciting moment, such as a near run-out, their falsetto screams sounded above the general hullaboloo. Competing ineffectively with the hubbub through-out the day, an officially appointed brass band could at times be heard, contributing (it goes without saying), selections from *The Gondoliers*.

But the great feature of Sydney cricket ground was, as it still is, the famous Hill. The match began on a Saturday and the whole place was packed out. Across the ground from where I was sitting was a vast conglomerated mass of humanity, as raucous then as it can ever have been since, though perhaps not so actively demonstrative. I didn't see any beer cans thrown but there was a fierce and constant chorus of animosity against any player they had marked down for displeasure. From the first this animosity was directed against Jardine. It was their first sight of him but he aroused in them what seemed to be an instinctive and contagious prejudice (his habitual Harlequin cap was a provocation in itself). The word must have got round that Jardine was a stiff-necked, high-nosed type of cove, as indeed he was. He opened the innings with Sutcliffe (Jack Hobbs wasn't playing) and in this, his third innings in Australia, made his third successive century. I was in the dressing-room when he was got out and Patsy Hendren was preparing to follow him in. Patsy said, 'They don't seem to like you very much over here, Mr Jardine.' To which Jardine replied, 'It's . . . mutual.' The blank was a participle which, however familiar nowadays, was beyond the bounds of refinement then—even in Australia.

England made a huge score. Hammond and Hendren made centuries as well as Jardine and Leyland, and Ames would have too if the innings had run its course. And it was here at Sydney that Bradman took that first toll of English bowling. I witnessed one rather striking incident during that innings of his. When Bradman made one particularly brilliant cover drive, an enthusiast sitting near me in the members' stand was so carried away that he rose to his feet and shouted, 'Trumper.' He was pulled violently back into his seat and for the moment appeared in danger of being lynched. However exultant his fellow members were about the Bowral boy, they remained devout in their worship of their old heroes. This was near blasphemy.

As I write about that week or so in Sydney—my initiation into cricket in Australia—I recapture the feeling of delectation it brought me, so far exceeding anything I had anticipated. I don't know whether it is so now—I hope it still is—but at any rate in those days when an England team was touring Australia, cricket, cricket, cricket was the one prevailing topic of interest, indeed of importance. And here was I, unexpectedly, intimately mixed up with it all—a cricket-lover's nirvana.

Brisbane in 1928 was still developing into the important modern city it has now become. In some quarters what were then the very latest in imposing modern buildings contrasted with a colony of streets, consisting of shack-like dwellings which looked as if they had been transported from a Hollywood Western. On one side of the hotel where we stayed was a recently-erected stately public building with tame kangaroos leaping between the palm trees in its spacious garden but the hotel itself must have hitherto escaped the attentions of the developers. I remember sitting with some of the team on its antiquated and ramshackle wooden veranda, politely enduring George Geary's efforts to entertain us on his ukelele. The bathroom facilities must have been pretty sketchy too. On the early morning of 30 November, when the first Test was to begin, I had to share a bath with Percy Chapman. Accustomed as I was to the extravagant practices of the theatre, I expected him to be in receipt of a sheaf of letters and cables from well-wishers in England, but the only communication he had received that morning was a reminder from the British Inland Revenue relating to his income tax. As I told him in the bathroom, England evidently expected that every man that day would pay his duty.

Like the hotel, the 1928 Brisbane cricket ground was somewhat behind the times in accommodation and appointment. I was given a seat in a small separate stand above the visiting

39

players' dressing-room, which was below ground level. There were none of the comparatively cultured amenities of Sydney—no privileged ladies' enclosure, no muted brass band. But whatever number of spectators the ground was supposed to hold, it must that morning have held a good few more than it was supposed to. And here was I, waiting to see the first ball bowled in a Test series in Australia.

I suppose it is because the feeling that that ambition, triggered off by good old P. F. Warner, was at last being fulfilled that the recollection of that first ball remains so clearly in my memory. Chapman had won the toss. Hobbs took guard and Jack Gregory began his splendid giant-stride run. Before he had gone two paces a great roaring thunder-clap of encouragement burst from all round the ring. The ball sped well outside the off-stump and Hobbs watched it with an air of respectful contemplation. He was the coolest—perhaps the only cool—man on the ground.

Hobbs possessed a marvellously even temperament. I never saw or heard him incensed or contentious. His wife was sitting near me and when he had been run out for 49 he came up to see her. He said, 'It was all my fault; I started late. I ought to have taken a taxi.'

England batted until tea-time on the second day and ran up a total of 521. Hendren made 169 and figured in a big seventh-wicket stand with Larwood, who made 70. The Australian bowling seemed well below standard. Apart from Gregory and Grimmett they relied chiefly on a left-arm slow bowler named Ironmonger, who was treated with a good deal of duplicity and encouragement by the English batsmen. He had a very suspect action and I remarked to Jardine, 'This chap, Ironmonger, looks to me as if he throws.' Jardine replied, 'Of course he throws. But don't, for God's sake, tell anybody so.'

England eventually won by the terrific margin of 675 runs. But Australia had to play the fourth innings on a wicket which had been visited by a rainstorm and Jack White cleaned the side up, taking four wickets for 7 runs. So it was all a very one-sided affair but for me it contained one feature which was never acclaimed as it should have been, namely the most amazing catch I ever saw. Right at the opening of Australia's first innings on the second evening of the match, Larwood began operating at full speed. Woodfull snicked him so many feet to the left of Percy Chapman in the gully that the ball looked to be far beyond his reach. Chapman took off like a swallow, reached the ball with his outstretched left hand, hung on to it somehow and was carried by his own impetus to fall past slips and wicket still holding it safely. I was not carried away by enthusiasm into over-estimating this astonishing stunt. Hobbs said it was the finest catch he had ever seen.

Bradman made 18 and 1 in this match and was dropped from the side for the second Test at Sydney—a shocking lapse of judgement on the part of the Australian selectors. He was reinstated for the third match at Melbourne and his scores in the last three Tests in this, his first season against England, were 79 and 112; 40 and run out 58; 123 and not out 37. Warren Bardsley, who was one of the selectors, was also a salesman of Yeast-Vite; so ardent a salesman that, later in the tour at a Government House dinner to both teams to which I was invited, Bardsley produced samples of Yeast-Vite and passed them down the table. Whether, after removing Bradman from the side, he stuffed him with Yeast-Vite in preparation for the third and future Tests I do not know, but if so it was a very good advertisement.

The only other memory I have of the Brisbane Test may seem very trifling, but it is so often the trivial incidents that do stick. At the end of the second day's play, when England had made their 521 and Australia had lost four wickets for next to nothing, I was leaving my stand and made way for a very pretty Australian girl, whom I had never seen before (my mind had been entirely upon cricket). She was evidently a keen cricket fan, soliloquising aloud and almost tearfully about the desperate state of things. I said to her, 'Oh, don't worry too much. Anything may happen. Cricket's a funny game.' She looked disdainfully at my M.C.C. tie. 'To you, it is,' she said.

The second Test at Sydney was a high-scoring match. In all, 1,302 runs were made for the loss of 32 wickets, an average of over 40 a wicket, but it was no lesser a walk-over for England than the Brisbane game had been. Australia's bowling was even weaker than before because Gregory had wrecked himself during the Brisbane match and took no further part in Tests from then on. Moreover, Archie Jackson, who had been coupled with Bradman as a dazzling prospect, was already a victim to the tuberculosis which was to cut short his career. He wasn't fit enough to play in this series until the fourth Test at Adelaide, when he made 164 and 30. If he had been granted health and strength he would have been one of the most prolific scorers Australia ever turned out. A graceful and stylish bats-man too, though, in this respect, there was never a batsman I watched with greater relish than Jackson's contemporary, Alan Kippax.

Kippax, on the opening day of this match, was the pro-tagonist of a long-forgotten, inflammatory incident. He was bowled by Geary for 9 but thought that the ball had rebounded off Duckworth's pads on to the wicket. The umpires, after much hesitant consultation, gave him out and all hell was let loose. The Hill, not unnaturally, shared Kippax's view. For the whole of the rest of the match, whenever he handled the ball, Duckworth was subjected to loud, tedious and sardonic barracking: 'Why don't yer kick the stumps down?' etc. George Duckworth thrived on it. At the end of England's first innings he put up a long tenth-wicket stand with Farmer White and emerged with 39 not out. I was with him soon afterwards and congratulated him. He gave me a beam of contentment. 'Aye,' he said, 'it's very sootisfactory when they have to come to you on their hands and knees.'

This was Walter Hammond's great tour. In the Sydney match he was only called upon to bat once and made 251. His subsequent Test scores were: 200 and run out 32; 119 and

177; 38 and 16. After this innings of 251 he showed me his bat. Nowadays in TV close-ups one sees bats festooned with the blots of impact. Hammond's bat was unmarked, except that plumb in the middle of the sweet of the blade there was a perfectly circular indentation.

During this match, and even in the course of his innings of 251, I spent a considerable time in Wally Hammond's company. Before I had set out from England I had bought a large and powerful pair of field-glasses. I have already said that a show-case of Sydney's beauty queens was to be seen just to the right of where I was sitting throughout the match. Hammond, not out at the luncheon break, or taking the appointed forty minutes off from first slip, as the case might be, would arrive at my side soon after the start of the interval. He would say nothing; merely hold out his hand for the field-glasses. There he would sit, the field-glasses making a detailed tour of the Ladies' Enclosure, until a few minutes before play was due to start again, when he would hand me back the field-glasses, say, 'Thanks,' and disappear. Laconic. But that was all part of his reserved and diffident nature. He was always very well disposed towards me and made me feel that he liked my being one of the party—quite apart from the field-glasses.

Once again the Australian barrackers kept monotonously and pointedly picking on Jardine as their prize butt. At one time, when he was fielding at deep third man, just in front of the Hill, he had to listen to a non-stop chorus of personal abuse. He took absolutely no notice until there was a change in the field and he had to end his spell in that position. Just before he left it, he half-turned his head, spat on the ground and moved off.

But if the Australian cricket spectators everywhere singled out Jardine for disfavour, they singled out Pat Hendren for their favouritism. He had been out there on two previous tours and had become adopted as Australia's pet English cricketer. He was always in deadly earnest when on the job; no one could have been more keyed up and determined but Nature had cast

43

him as a comedian and he was always subjected to a good deal of badinage along with the cheers. He was also a tremendous asset to the side when off-duty. Phil Mead used to follow him around like an old pet dog.

It was during this match that I first met the man who was to become one of my greatest friends in the cricket world. Arthur Mailey had been debarred from playing for Australia in this series because he had taken up a job as a reporter and cartoonist covering the Tests for a Sydney paper. We became definite, permanent friends almost from the moment we first met and we remained so, whether we saw much of each other or not, all through the next forty years until he died. I have a good deal more to say about him, but I had better put that off and carry on with my tour. There's not much more that need be said about this second Test. England totalled 636, with every man on the side making double figures. Australia made 397 in their second knock and this left us with only 16 to make to win. Chapman gave his tail-enders the mild task of securing the 16 and here followed an episode which I think has never before been revealed. Probably it was thought to be so greatly to the detriment of those concerned that it had better be suppressed.

Some sportive Australian cove, a bookmaker perhaps, sent a message to the England dressing-room offering five pounds to any batsman who hit a six in the course of making the sixteen runs. George Geary and Maurice Tate were the opening pair and both fell for this alluring offer, but Tate was caught by Bradman fielding sub for Ponsford for 4 and Geary took a swipe at Hendry and was bowled for 8. Both were quite unrepentant at having had a bash for the fiver and Chapman was not the captain to reprimand them, beyond having a good laugh at their expense.

On the Sunday of this match there was a charity game on a suburban ground. Three or four of the greatest Australian former players consented to participate and Arthur Mailey insisted that I was roped in. I agreed on condition I was sent in number eleven. I was provided with a bat so heavy that I could scarcely lift it but was encouraged on my way to the wicket with some shouts of 'Rookery Nook' from the spectators. Clem Hill used the opportunity to experiment and bowled deliveries at me, some of which ascended some forty feet in the air, but I survived at 1 not out.

And so, with the first two Test matches well in the bottom of the bag, the England team moved on to Melbourne for the third. Of all the England v. Australia Tests I ever watched, this Melbourne match, which started on 29 December 1928, was all things considered the greatest, even though Jessop's match must seem the most exciting in its closing stages.

It has never been acclaimed as such by the historians, due no doubt to the fact that English historians never watched it, but only heard and read about it, and to Australian historians it meant the loss of the Ashes—and was morosely played down accordingly. So I feel justified in dealing in rather more detail with the actual course of play in this match than with the two previous encounters. Moreover, it contained one or two background incidents which, at the moment of writing, only Leslie Ames, Harold Larwood, George Geary and myself still live to remember.

Since those days the Melbourne ground has been entirely reconstructed to make the vast stadium it is today, which I have visited on two or three occasions. In 1928 it could hold a capacity crowd of about seventy thousand. On the first day it beat all previous records for a cricket match anywhere in the world. Some daring spirits took a precarious perch on the shaky-looking roof of one of the wooden beerstalls. On the second morning I arrived in company with Victor Richardson, the cheeriest and most convivial of all the Australian side. As he surveyed another teeming full-house he remarked to me, 'Hullo. Not so many people here yet—there's no one on top of the soaker.'

Rather than stay away on that first morning, mothers in scores brought their babies with them. Several parked them over the picket-fences and play was held up on a number of occasions while the umpire proceeded to the boundary to pick up a baby and restore it firmly to its owner.

Kippax was again the central figure early on; but not, this time, because of a disputed decision—far from it. Australia had won the toss and lost two cheap wickets. This bad start had depressed the crowd which, like some gigantic animal, seemed all the more churlish because of its huge size. Larwood had got one of the early wickets and was at his most menacing. Kippax went for him and, like Jessop of old, hit him for three 4's to long on off successive balls. The crowd woke up and went crazy. The men shouted, the women screamed and the babies yelled. Kippax sobered down but went on to make exactly 100 and Ryder, the Australian captain, at number five, made 112. Number seven was no less a reprieved batsman than Bradman, who, fortified perhaps by Bardsley's Yeast-Vite, made 79 before being bowled by Hammond. Incidentally, Bradman once told me that of all the English bowlers on that trip he found Hammond the most difficult to tackle.

Despite all this, Australia made only 397. Farmer White kept them boxed up at one end anyhow. He bowled 30 maidens out of his 57 overs, an astonishing performance on a plum Melbourne wicket. England topped them by twenty runs on the first innings, but this was largely due to Hammond who made 200. Jardine made 62 and Sutcliffe 58 but none of the others reached 25. So the third innings started at pretty well all square.

On the next day the England side had to endure by far the toughest ordeal of the tour so far. It was a day of sweltering humidity, working up slowly for a good old Australian thunderstorm. But this did not arrive until just before the close by which time Australia had lost about six wickets. Woodfull settled in and when Woodfull settled in it would have taken King Kong to unsettle him. He was eventually out for 107 but even so he was not the chief trouble. Once more I was privileged to witness an historic occasion—Bradman's first century

46

against England. It wasn't the circumspect, questing innings of one ambitious to establish himself for the days to come, it was the already arrived, completely confident, rampaging Bradman of the future. Then, at the end of the day, with Australia already well over 200 ahead the heavens opened and the rain fell on the uncovered wicket as if from one immeasurable overturned bucket.

Next morning the sun was blazing as strongly as ever. It not merely dried out the sodden wicket; it scorched it. Play was delayed for an hour or more while it did so. By that time no batsman could hope to survive on such an assassin of a strip. Jack White polished off the Australian tail-enders almost mechanically. Hobbs and Sutcliffe managed to struggle through the few remaining minutes before the luncheon interval. Hobbs, as he came back to the dressing-room, was resigned but characteristically placid. 'Well, there it is,' he said. 'I'm afraid it'll be all over before tea-time.'

I had been invited to lunch with the President of the Victorian Cricket Association. All the old nabobs were there, the Trumbles and Nobles and Hills. They were all very genial in their undisguised elation and jocular in their sympathy towards me, representing England. I was with the assistant secretary of the Association after lunch, when the officer in charge of the police arrangements came up and asked him about how many of his men would be wanted on the ground next day. Next day? The assistant secretary laughed him to scorn. He couldn't know much about cricket. This sounded like a challenge and called for an Australian measure of retaliation. I was appointed witness to the bet which was on level terms. No, the police officer couldn't know much about cricket.

In that radio interview at Lord's, I was asked what I thought was the best innings I'd ever seen. I replied the innings of 49 played by Jack Hobbs that day. During its scorching period the wicket became pitted and furrowed into horrid corrugated patches which soon became baked as hard as concrete. Every ball of whatever pace or length was a fresh, unpredictable

ENGLAND PLAYING ON A BUMPY WICKET.

A WET WICKET —

A MUDDY WICKET—

—AND A SUNNY WICKET ALL IN THE SAME GAME.

LANCE MATTINSON

GOT AWAY WITH THE ASHES. MIND YOU, I THINK MELBOURNE WAS FOOLISH IN PROVIDING ENGLAND WITH SUCH TYPICAL ENGLISH CONDITIONS!

menace, the bowlers themselves couldn't foretell what last split-second antic it might perform. Throughout the whole afternoon and early evening Hobbs and Sutcliffe gave an extraordinary exhibition of skill and concentration and last-moment adjustment. Hobbs took charge and kept the strike whenever possible but perhaps it was Sutcliffe's dexterity and unruffled temperament that made Hobbs appear the senior partner. There were twenty-nine extras in the innings, and this with Oldfield keeping wicket. Even a good length ball was apt to leap up almost vertically and fly over Oldfield's head. Halfway through his innings Hobbs signalled for another bat, but this was only to send a message to Chapman to let Jardine come in at number three. They stuck it out until about an hour before close of play, when Hobbs was lbw for his 49 but Sutcliffe was still there with Jardine at the end of the day, and went on next morning to make 135 when the wicket had rolled out into comparative placidity. The bitterly disappointed and disgruntled Australian public and press were not very sporting about the monumental Hobbs-Sutcliffe effort. When Sutcliffe, halfway through his innings returned in the evening to the members' enclosure, he had to turn his head to see where the solitary applause was coming from and he and I exchanged a grin.

Jardine took me out that evening to have a look at what they'd been batting on and I haven't in the least exaggerated in my description of the wicket, any more than I have exaggerated in saying that I had seen that day the finest innings that I have ever had the nerve-racking, jitters-in-every-ball privilege of watching.

Though, as I have said, the last-day wicket was comparatively placid, it was nevertheless pretty spiteful and England had still quite a long way to go in order to make the 332 wanted to win. 'Oh,' Pat Hendren said to me in his most earnest, prayerful tone, 'how I would love to make 50 today.' He made 45 and after a hectic last half-hour we scraped home by three wickets. As George Geary made the winning hit I was standing between Beat Chapman and Jack Hobbs and we all flung our

MELBOURNE

December 1928–January 1929

AUSTRALIA

	1st inns		2nd inns	
W. M. Woodfull	c. Jardine b. Tate	3	c. Duckworth b. Tate	107
V. Y. Richardson	c. Duckworth b. Larwood	3	b. Larwood	5
H. L. Hendry	c. Jardine b. Larwood	23	st. Duckworth b. White	12
A. F. Kippax	c. Jardine b. Larwood	100	b. Tate	41
J. Ryder	c. Hendren b. Tate	112	b. Geary	5
D. G. Bradman	b. Hammond	79	c. Duckworth b. Geary	112
W. A. Oldfield	b. Geary	3	b. White	7
E. L. a'Beckett	c. Duckworth b. White	41	b. White	6
R. K. Oxenham	b. Geary	15	b. White	39
C. V. Grimmett	c. Duckworth b. Geary	5	not out	4
D. D. J. Blackie	not out	3	b. White	0
	Extras	7	Extras	13
	Total	397	Total	351

Bowling	O.	M.	R.	W.	O.	M.	R.	W.
Larwood	37	3	127	3	16	3	37	1
Tate	48	17	87	2	48	15	70	2
Geary	31	14	83	3	30	4	94	2
Hammond	8	4	19	1	16	6	30	0
White	57	30	64	1	56.2	20	107	5
Jardine	1	0	10	0	—	—	—	—

ENGLAND

	1st inns		2nd inns	
J. B. Hobbs	c. Oldfield b. a'Beckett	20	l.b.w. b. Blackie	49
H. Sutcliffe	b. Blackie	58	l.b.w. b. Grimmett	135
W. Hammond	c. a'Beckett b. Blackie	200	run out	32
A. P. F. Chapman	b. Blackie	24	c. Woodfull b. Ryder	5
E. Hendren	c. a'Beckett b. Hendry	19	b. Oxenham	45
D. R. Jardine	c. & b. Blackie	62	b. Grimmett	33
H. Larwood	c. & b. Blackie	0		
G. Geary	l.b.w. b. Grimmett	1	not out	4
G. Duckworth	b. Blackie	3	not out	0
M. W. Tate	c. Kippax b. Grimmett	21	run out	0
J. C. White	not out	8		
	Extras	1	Extras	29
	Total	417	Total (for 7 wickets)	332

Bowling	O.	M.	R.	W.	O.	M.	R.	W.
a'Beckett	27	7	92	1	22	5	39	0
Hendry	20	8	35	1	23	5	33	0
Grimmett	55	14	114	2	35	12	96	2
Oxenham	27	11	67	0	28	10	44	1
Blackie	44	13	94	6	39	11	75	1
Ryder	4	0	14	0	5.5	1	16	1

England won by 3 wickets

50

arms around each other. England had won the Ashes. And the police officer had long since won his bet.

There is another good reason why that Test of fifty years ago remains more endearing to me than any of the many I have attended in both countries since. Recap the close of play on that dreadful third evening, when the England team had spent the day in a steam oven, striving to grapple with the irremovable Woodfull and the irrepressible Bradman and, to crown all, with the preliminary clots of rain falling on them, spelling certain defeat, as they left the field. I was with Maurice Leyland, the twelfth man, in the dressing-room as they trooped in, utterly exhausted, dripping with sweat and, for once, dispirited and inclined to be acrimonious. Somebody had to put things to rights. There was only one man who could do it.

In the course of the stripping and cooling-off stage, Patsy Hendren, sitting stark naked, began to imitate a monkey searching the more likely portions of its anatomy for fleas. Within a couple of minutes he had everybody roaring with laughter. A little later he managed somehow to intercept the driver of a large horse-drawn van which had been unloading an immense cargo of beer for the morrow and to commission him to drive the England side back to the hotel. Aboard the van, Patsy gave an imitation of a bus conductor on a par with his monkey. Everybody landed back at the hotel in the best of spirits. Of all the cricketers I ever knew, major or minor, Patsy Hendren was blessed with the supreme gift of natural bonhomie and of an infectious, optimistic outlook. His average as a batsman in the Tests of this tour 52.44. His average as a member of the team was incalculable.

Patsy's generosity of spirit was not quite so evident in one other member of the team. Some enthusiast in England cabled the gift of one hundred pounds each to Hobbs and Sutcliffe. This, temporarily at any rate, infuriated Wally Hammond. And, after all, it had been his 200 in the first innings which had accounted for England having been left with the semblance of a chance from then on. 'I'm not going to make any more bloody hundreds,' he said to me bitterly. In the next Test at Adelaide he made two of them, so his rancour didn't last long.

On the very day when his third Test Match ended I, too, received a cable from England. Oh, damn; they wanted me back to get busy with the next Aldwych farce. But no 'oh, damn' really. I wanted to be home again with my wife and family and I had accompanied the best England side that ever toured Australia while they won the Ashes in three straight matches, in the capacity of an accepted hobnobber. My friendship with many of them was to continue over the years ahead. But, above all, it had been on this, my first visit to Australia, that I had got to know Arthur Mailey.

Four

Bradman, Grimmett and Co.

One fruitful result of my summons back to the Aldwych was that in the summer of 1930 I was at liberty to watch all the five Tests here in England from start to finish. Arthur was over here doing his reporting; once more I was received back into the England fold—my wife and I had seen a good deal of the Chapmans in the meantime. Again my memories of fifty years ago outshine anything in the cricket world that has happened since. And again, this having been the first of the several amazing visitations of Bradman upon England, the tour figures prominently in the history books and there is no need for me to dwell on what went on in the middle. All I want to do is to recall a few of the personal encounters and incidents.

On the first morning of the opening Test at Trent Bridge I found myself seated beside a chap I knew slightly and admired greatly, the celebrated A. A. Milne, who was like myself a great lover of cricket. At one point he gave me a shrewd example of his witty line of thought. He turned to me and said, 'The sound of Hobbs' bat puts me in mind of vintage port.' A perfect simile, though Jack Hobbs wouldn't have appreciated it as I did. He was a strict non-bibber.

This was the only Test which England won in that series. Walter Robins, a very cheerful, confident character, put England well on top after an innings each (50 not out and 4 for 51). When Australia were left with 429 to win, their only hope was to make a draw of it and so they would have if McCabe, going strong with Bradman, hadn't been the victim of that historic catch by one of the Notts ground staff, Copley, who was substituting for Sutcliffe. As it was, England won by 93.

53

I am ashamed to say I missed the Copley catch. On my arrival in Nottingham I had struck up what was to be a close friendship with Tom Webster, whose *Daily Mail* cartoons covering all manner of sport were unapproached in originality and popularity by a host of copy-cats. He had never been keen on cricket but became so, as he always told me, when I enlightened him and took him along to get to know some of the players. He had to go back to London on the last morning of the match to cover a fight for the heavyweight championship. He persuaded me to go with him. I am glad I yielded, because, although I missed the Copley catch, it entailed my one and only interview with Ranji, who by now had become HH the Maharajah Jam Sahib of Nawanagar. He was giving a party that evening to both teams and others and had invited me along. So I had to go and beg leave off. I found him seated in his private suite at his hotel. He looked rather formidable and, I thought, affronted, as with some trepidation I prayed to be excused his invitation. 'The fact is, Jam Sahib, that Tom Webster wants me to go and see the big fight with him in London tonight.' Ranji's expression changed into a broad smile. He replied in a confidential undertone : 'Oh, Mr Travers,' he said, 'between ourselves, I only wish I could come with you.'

The Lord's Test that year is another which has been well chronicled. It began with Frank Woolley going in first with Hobbs and treating the Australian bowlers like prep school boys—making 41 while Hobbs made only one. Ranji's nephew, Duleepsinhji, came in when we had lost two wickets. I was sitting with Tom Webster. Tom was a very self-reliant character. He was continuously being pestered by chuckling suggesters of 'good ideas' for his cartoons and hated the sight of them. I was never a suggester but this was one of the two occasions when some remark of mine formed the basis of a *Daily Mail* cartoon. This depicted Duleep approaching the wicket seated on an Indian elephant with Uncle Ranji leading the elephant and issuing instructions to his nephew, using the trunk as a telephone.

Duleep made 173 in the Lord's Test. He was a delightful batsman; better than Uncle Ranji, though to say so was like telling the old Australian pundits that Bradman was better than Trumper. Duleep didn't possess some of Ranji's subtleties, such as tickling a ball to long leg from under rather than round his left leg, but if he had only had decent health there's no knowing what his record would have been. I was with Duleep at Taunton a few years later when he played his last innings before being packed off to hospital. He made 90 odd and said to me wistfully, 'Oh, if only I had been well.' He was the most gracious-mannered, courteous cricketer imaginable. Duleep and Archie Jackson—two great cricket careers cut short. Whom the Gods love die young.

It was as well Duleep made his 173. Hobbs and Hammond had gone by the luncheon interval on that first morning. During the break, I caught sight of a figure who brought me nostalgic fascination and furtive amusement. Parading up and down in front of the pavilion was no less an elderly virtuoso than A. C. MacLaren. He was carrying a tightly-rolled umbrella, with which he was illustrating to Ranji the various cricket strokes required for dealing with such as Grimmett. There he was, over thirty years since I had last seen him, the same domineering personality.

On the Sunday of that match I played golf with Tom Webster against Victor Richardson and Alan Kippax. The latter had joined Bradman at the wicket in the late evening with only about half an hour's play still to go. Bradman had by that time made a goodly proportion of his 254 and, being Bradman, had only thoughts for the morrow. Kippax confided to me his utter, bottled-up resentment of Bradman, who had taken good care that he, Kippax, the newcomer, had to take the strike whenever possible. Bradman's Test record on that tour (7 innings; 974 runs. Highest score 334; average 139.14) undoubtedly raised jealousy in the Australian camp, Woodfull apart. This was in contrast to the England side's admiration for Hammond on the recent tour of Australia, when the only

55

member of the side to display any jealousy had been Hammond himself. But then in the England side, with such characters as Percy Chapman, Pat Hendren, Maurice Leyland and George Duckworth, there had always been a prevailing sense of humour, something that was conspicuously lacking in this Australian side—apart from Vic Richardson, that is.

COMING EVENTS CAST THEIR SHADOWS AT OLD TRAFFORD OR—
— THE ENGLISH CAPTAIN SEES SOMETHING "FUNNY" ABOUT THE WICKET.

After the defeat at Lord's came the Leeds Test in which Bradman made 300 on the first day and, although Hammond made another century, and England totalled 391 we had to follow on. Rain interfered, the match was drawn and we went on to Manchester all square. It is this Manchester Test which lingers in my memory, not because of the cricket—more rain and another draw—but because of some of the side issues.

The cricket itself was chiefly notable for the introduction into the England side of Ian Peebles with his leg-spin and googlies which baffled Bradman and had him caught at slip by Duleep for only 14. But there was another cricket incident of which I alone know the nub. Australia were all out on the second morning and Hobbs and Sutcliffe were padded up waiting to go in. I was in the dressing-room talking to Sutcliffe when somebody delivered the official list of the team selected to tour South Africa in the forthcoming winter. To everybody's astonishment Sutcliffe had been omitted. Sandham had been chosen to be Hobbs' opening partner.

Sutcliffe, having regularly opened with Hobbs, was acutely aware of his status. The reception of this news drove him instantly into a paroxysm of refined fury. 'Sand *ham*' he demanded of me—in his very refined 'u' voice. 'Who is Sand *ham*?' (He had been with Andy Sandham on the 1924–5 tour to Australia.) Next moment he was called upon to go out and bat. Whether still giving vent to his fume or to show the selectors what he thought of them, I don't know. But from the start he ran amok, flailing the bowlers in all directions heedless of risk and leaving Hobbs standing. Even when he was caught at long leg for 74 he declared that Bradman was over the boundary line and that he'd really hit a six, but Bradman and the umpire ruled against him. However, none of the pressmen nor anybody but myself seemed to cotton on to what had given Herbert Sutcliffe this dazzling uncharacteristic impetus.

Some Mancunian big-pot invited the two teams and all-and-sundry connected with the Test to a Sunday afternoon party on his spacious neighbouring estate. During this function Arthur Mailey got into trouble with the somewhat cross-grained manager of the Australian team. Arthur had been fascinated by Ian Peebles' success and, taking Peebles on one side, he engaged him in a matey private exchange of views on spin and googly bowling and the methods employed. The manager angrily accused Arthur of giving Peebles hints and, I think, reported him to his newspaper editor in Australia. Not that Arthur cared a damn. All that concerned him was the pleasure of discovering a kindred spirit and fellow performer—no matter where he came from.

Arthur, to his own chuckling relish, found himself in further disfavour with his countrymen that afternoon. Tom Webster and I challenged him and Clarrie Grimmett to a set of lawn tennis in shirtsleeves and socks and most of the Aussie side gathered eagerly to stand by and watch the kill. Tom and I won 6–0 and the onlookers drifted away quite seriously mortified. The inherent Australian will to win never lets up.

There was a brief stoppage for rain on the last evening of this Oval match and, quite by chance, I spent most of it with Bill Woodfull, the Australian captain, a congenial character, rather of the Noble type, serious and immensely shrewd. I sounded him about Grimmett who, in these Tests, had been a menace to England second only to Bradman. Grimmett's figures for the five Tests didn't look much on paper—29 wickets at 31.89 a wicket; but ever since the first morning at Trent Bridge, when he had bowled Hammond for 8, got Frank Woolley first ball and tied Pat Hendren up in knots before bowling him for 5, once the shine was off the ball, Woodfull would beckon Grimmett in from cover point to come and take over. Then, all round the ground, there would come a rippling buzz of foreboding, occasionally justified, always justifiable. Woodfull had become familiar with that buzz and had enjoyed the right of deciding when to press the button.

Nearly forty years later in 1967 I spent a whole day at Adelaide watching a Test with Grimmett, by then a wizened, rather cross-grained little old man. He still bore a lasting grudge against Bertie Oldfield, who had universally been regarded as the best wicket-keeper ever until Godfrey Evans came along. Grimmett asserted that if he had had Tallon behind the stumps throughout his career he would have got twice as many wickets, a surprising and sweeping statement;

but then Clarrie Grimmett was always a bit of a sweeper both by nature and in his bowling action.

Grimmett and Mailey were Australia's two greatest slow bowlers to appear on the scene since the days of Hugh Trumble, though H. V. Hordern had one brief and remarkable spell in the England tour of 1911–12 (32 wickets at an average of 24.37). Grimmett played with Mailey in only four Tests against England, in which he took 24 wickets to Mailey's 14. As a mere watcher I cannot, of course, compare their respective methods and tactics but as regards their personalities and characteristics there can never have been a greater contrast between two spin bowlers. Mailey was a hunter; Grimmett a sharp-shooter. Mailey looked on the ball as his friend. Grimmett looked on the ball as his servant.

But what really mattered at Manchester was what used to take place at the hotel after dinner. Percy Chapman and some of the team with Tom Webster and myself, would foregather in the lounge. Maurice Tate was always the centre of attraction. In cricket circles he was almost as renowned for his solecisms and malapropisms as he was for his bowling. But he was always unabashed and forthcoming and was the first to join in the laughter which was admittedly pretty loud and long at times. Chapman was never given a hint that these proceedings were regarded with great disfavour by the selectors. They couldn't and didn't have any suspicions or accusations as regards the booze : they simply didn't think that Percy Chapman was conducting himself as an England captain should. The result was that he was given the sack. When the team for the Oval was announced he was out and Bob Wyatt appointed captain.

This caused a public sensation and, although nothing came out in the press about the Manchester after-dinner coteries, I was told that a prominent Middlesex amateur, a disciple no doubt of Plum Warner, was heard to snort his contempt for 'Tom Webster and Ben Travers, the two who lost England the Ashes'. This pleased me (and Arthur Mailey) enormously. Firstly it made me feel stuck-up to be told I counted that much;

secondly it must go down as the silliest comment ever made about cricket, beating anything that even Maurice Tate had to offer.

No, the gentleman who lost the Ashes for England on that tour was D. G. Bradman, as he demonstrated at the Oval in the first of the two terrific second-wicket partnerships he was to share with Ponsford on that ground. Although England made 405 (Sutcliffe 161, just to give the selectors another kick up the behind) and 251, we lost by an innings and 39 runs. The *Daily Mail* had been on the alert to take advantage of Chapman's dismissal and had offered him a thousand pounds to contribute his report of the match day by day. On the first morning, still among his fond adherents in their dressing-room, sitting with a pad on his knee and a blank writing-pad on the shin-pad, he implored me to stick by him and write the damn stuff for him to send in. In view of what eventually appeared I hasten to state that I declined his plea.

Paradoxically, Percy Chapman was ordered off-field solely because it was off-field that his merry deportment as captain offended the selectors. On-field no captain could have made a more successful job in doing his best to restrict the tidal-wave of runs which swamped our Test grounds in that Bradman season. Chapman's own batting efforts contributed handsomely to any retaliation England had to offer. In our first innings at Trent Bridge he had saved England's prestige with a cracking 49 and did so to an even greater extent with his second innings century at Lord's. In his one knock in the drawn game at Leeds he made 45. For his six Test innings in the series his average was 43.16. So his sacking must have been an act of what my children's old Nanny used to refer to as 'dipsipline'.

The selectors were Percy Perrin (always known as Peter Perrin for some reason), Frank Mann, the Middlesex captain, and Farmer White. The latter had been Chapman's vice-captain in Australia and I can't understand his concurrence, but perhaps he was out-voted. If they or any other selectors consider that a spirit of friendly, cheerful, laughing optimism

61

puts a chap out of commission as a cricket captain, I don't. But then I'm only an onlooker and they know better than I do. Or do they?

As all Percy Chapman's old acquaintances know, the finish of his cricket career brought about a sad change in his hitherto happy nature; but nothing can detract from the felicitous memories I have of him as a cricketer and a friend. In his time there was no more flamboyant middle-order attacking batsman and in all my experience as a cricket watcher I have never known a better all-round fielder or one more gifted with the anticipation and ability to hang on to an almost impossible catch.

Five

The Jardine Interlude

The ensuing 1930–31 England tour in Australia retains a chapter to itself in the cricket history books—the famous or infamous 'body-line' series. No tour has ever been more written about, debated and table-thumped about, very little more can be usefully contributed by an old stay-at-home who had it all at second-hand. All I can say, as eye-witness of Jardine's previous experiences in Australia, is that it was asking for trouble and an initial diplomatic blunder to send him out there as skipper of a Test side. The animosity which perpetually simmered within him towards Australia was in no way lessened by the knowledge of the kind of reception awaiting him. On the contrary this only went to keep the animosity on the bubble. His astute mind concentrated on devising a means of getting his own back, with the Ashes as a convincing exhibit on the side.

Fortune favoured him with the weapons essential for his purpose. Voce was a formidable collaborator—corresponding in a way to what Sutcliffe had been to Hobbs—but Larwood could be a killer.

When the Australians came over here in 1934, Percy Chapman and I managed to persuade Bill Woodfull to come alone to dinner on the second night after their arrival. We asked him to give us the low-down on the whole story of the 'body-line' business. He didn't want to go into the ethics of the thing, he was sick of all that; but he rather surprised us by saying that it wasn't first and foremost the ethics that mattered so much—the Australians could have dealt with them. The real problem was the terrific pace at which Larwood sent down that short-pitched ball. Woodfull had, of course, played Larwood many times before in both countries and all the other fast bowlers on offer, but he had never known anything like the speed that Larwood worked up on that tour. There wasn't an atom of time to get out of the way of it unless you walked away to leg (as Ponsford did) and exposed your stumps. Woodfull himself and Bert Oldfield both got a crack on the head and that was what chucked a bucket of petrol on the flames. Bill Woodfull was a gentle, generous-hearted man and what his summary really amounted to was a tribute to Larwood's capacity for obeying orders. But I wonder what old Tom Richardson would have had to say about it. He didn't knock them on the head; he bowled them out. In good old Somerset parlance, 'Give I Richardson.'

And so for Douglas Jardine : he was a Wykehamist. Whenever you sit next to a stranger at a club or dinner-party, who proves to be excellent company, but whose opinions are superior to yours and somebody tells you that he was at Winchester, your immediate reaction is, 'Ah, that accounts for it.' I have hitherto portrayed Douglas Jardine in rather a bad light, but of all the cricket celebrities I have known he stands apart. In many ways he was the heir to MacLaren. When we were in Australia he declined to sit at the same breakfast table as the pros, whereas Chapman was sitting and joking with them. One evening, when he walked into the Sports Club and saw me dining with a girl-friend he came, uninvited and joined us. My girl-friend was an Australian and became terrified that she would be boycotted by all her Australian friends for having been seen associating with Douglas Jardine. Nevertheless he had some admirable qualities : he was completely fearless and he possessed a witty, if somewhat sardonic, sense of humour. He died comparatively young, at fifty-eight, and I liked to picture his arrival at the Golden Gates, waving their custodians aside to make way for him, and warning them that if there was any argument about it he'd send for Larwood.

In the early 1930s my Aldwych farces were still going strong.

I invited Jack Hobbs and his wife to the opening night of one of them—in March 1932. On such occasions audiences had become accustomed to spotting social and theatrical celebrities in their midst but the presence of Jack Hobbs was regarded as a windfall by the public and press. He was almost mobbed in the vestibule and headlined in some of the morning papers—'Jack Hobbs as first-nighter'—and so on, as if he were the chief attraction of the evening, which perhaps he was. Oh, well; it wasn't the first time that Jack Hobbs had stolen the show. It was a nice tribute to his popularity, anyhow.

By the end of that year the body-line controversy had become a topic of such general interest that I made bold to set the scene of the next Aldwych farce, *A Bit of a Test*, in Sydney and in the thick of a Test Match. I say that I made bold because there were, and are, many who think there can be nothing funny about cricket—a mumpish point of view in my humble opinion. Playgoers of riper years will remember my Aldwych star comedians, Ralph Lynn, Robertson Hare and Mary Brough. My boldness knew no bounds in making Robertson Hare England's captain and Ralph Lynn England's star batsman. Both, not out on the Saturday evening, were lured by miscreants to go and spend the Sunday in the bush (*cherchez la femme*, of course) with the idea of holding them captive there until after they were due to resume their innings on Monday morning. But even the leading villain could not resist the seduction of a cricket conversation and spontaneously handed over his kosh in order that Ralph Lynn might demonstrate a stroke. Mary Brough, in riding breeches and boots, completed the rescue.

The farce was thought very funny except in Australia. When some optimist subsequently produced it down under it was regarded as a public scandal and quickly slain. I am glad I was not in Australia at the time or I might have been killed too.

It was at about this time that the first 'talkies' arrived to revolutionise the motion-picture business and to drive the old silent 'flicks' into oblivion. I was involved from the very start and became so occupied in the film studios that I had little time left for watching cricket. I had to give up any idea of going around to grounds outside London; but I managed to get to Lord's for the final day of the 1934 match, when the Australians were left stranded on a ruined wicket and Verity got his 7 for 61 and 8 for 43. I also took time off to watch the whole of the Oval match that year and had the delectation of witnessing Ponsford make 266 and Bradman 244 at the start of the game. This was the match in which Leslie Ames who, with the assistance of Maurice Leyland, was well on the way to rescuing England from the depths, when he was overtaken with virulent lumbago. As a result, throughout the Australian second innings, we had to endure the compassionate ordeal of watching Frank Woolley keeping wicket—a sad end to Ames' greatness as a Test player. The third highest contribution to the Australian total was 50 extras.

I was still busy when the Australians next came over in 1938 and could only manage one day at Lord's plus the whole of the Oval match. By this time a number of new and, in some cases, very distinguished performers had become recognised stars on both sides: Hutton, Compton, Edrich, Farnes; Lindsay Hassett, O'Reilly, W. A. Brown. The last-named carried his bat for 206 not out in the Lord's match; but I saw only the first day when Hammond played what is generally regarded as the greatest innings of his career : 240 after England had lost three cheap wickets. Eddie Paynter shared in a big partnership with him before getting out for 99. Anyone who watched the Oval match will look back on it as the greatest anticlimax in cricket. By the time Hutton, preferred at the last minute to Fagg, had finished making 364 and England 903 for 7, both Bradman and Fingleton had crocked themselves in the field and couldn't bat, which gave Australia's defeat by the margin of an innings and 579 a smack of absurdity.

It was now within one year of the outbreak of the Second World War and nearly all the players on both sides were complete strangers to me, but Bradman and Stan McCabe were still in the party and, with Arthur Mailey always around during a Test tour, I got to know some of the new Australian lads. Of these I found their wicket-keeper, Ben Barnett, the pick of the bunch, but only too soon he was destined, as a prisoner-of-war, to endure the brutal rigours of the Burma Road. When an English newspaper reported his survival and safe return home I sent him an overnight cable; but, not knowing where on earth he lived, I addressed the cable: 'Ben Barnett, Wicket-keeper, Australia.' I was sure it would reach him without delay and of course it did. I always think of it as a pleasing example of the appeal which cricket has to the average Australian.

Before the war, I often took the opportunity to spend a day at Lord's, watching county cricket. A few special occasions still delight my memory: August 15, 1925 Middlesex v. Notts. Notts win the toss. Enter George Gunn and takes strike against Gubby Allen, bowling from the Nursery end. As Allen begins his run, Gunn starts his walk down the wicket. He is a quarter way down it by the time the ball arrives to be hit for four on the full toss. This happens with the first four balls of the over. It can't be allowed to go on of course. Gubby bowls a high full toss over Gunn's head to the wicket-keeper and George Gunn has to return to the pavilion, stumped for 18 off the fifth ball of the first over. But what a character.

The second time was in the season immediately following the body-line controversy. (The visiting West Indians tried it against Jardine himself, who withstood it absolutely unflinching and speechless and took a century off them.) Some of the county fast bowlers were observed to be trying their luck with body-line and the press was on to it. A practical and satirical reaction is called for. To everybody's uproarious appreciation Patsy Hendren marches solemnly to the wicket wearing a motorcyclist's crash-helmet. A topical and practical gesture. Now he is at liberty to mock them or hook them or both.

At the time, it was treated as a characteristic and innocuous joke on Patsy's part. We might have thought very differently had we known that it was to be the prototype of the deplorable headgear seen in the cricket world of today.

Fortune has always been kind in planting me on the right spot to witness outstanding performances. I saw Arthur Wellard on one of the two occasions when he hit five sixes off consecutive balls. I saw Percy Fender make one of his under-the-hour centuries at the Oval. Incidentally, there continues to this day the preposterous system of reckoning and rewarding fast centuries by the clock, instead of by the number of deliveries received. Whole minutes of an eager batsman's time may be absorbed by bowlers who find it necessary to take a forty-yard run and, in many cases, indulge in a Weary Willie stroll back to their base.

For many years after the war I stuck to my cricket-watching as enthusiastically as ever and saw many of the London Tests against all-comers; some of them memorable. For example the Watson-Bailey match against Australia at Lord's in 1953 and that West Indian match in 1963 with its David Allen v. Wesley Hall final over, with Colin Cowdrey swathed in voluminous bandages at the other end. But I had lost contact with the cricketers themselves except for occasional meetings with old associates. I used to winter abroad (I was on my own now, having sadly lost my wife in 1951) and visited Australia several times. One of these visits coincided with the 1962–3 England tour which made it the most enjoyable experience since the old pre-war times. Together with Arthur Mailey, I watched three of the Tests. This was a notable period as both sides contained some of the greatest players I ever saw : Dexter, Cowdrey, Graveney, Trueman and Statham; Neil Harvey, R. B. Simpson, Benaud and Davidson, to say nothing of such support characters as David Sheppard, Titmus, Barrington, Illingworth, David Allen and J. T. Murray; Burke and Burge, Mackay, O'Neill, Booth and G. D. McKenzie.

Every important incident in each Test of that series has been covered in Ray Robinson's admirable contribution to the magnificent and monumental *Barclay's World of Cricket* recently published in the new edition, supervised by Jim Swanton and John Woodcock, of which I am the proud owner of a gift copy. And in any case it is cricket personalities I am concerned with. On this tour I not only met up with some of my pre-war friends—Vic Richardson, Bertie Oldfield and others—but, while at Adelaide, I was the guest of Don Bradman at a dinner-party at his house—an exclusive dinner-party, since the only other guests were Arthur Mailey and Bradman's two fellow selectors, one of whom was Jack Ryder. I was regarded as a privileged and reliable auditor of their discussions on this, the second evening of the Test, and I was given the opportunity of taking stock of Don as cricket's legislator rather than its supreme expert. His success in both capacities tends to obscure the fact that he possesses a brain which would have got him anywhere in any walk of life. His personality and manner have something akin to his batsmanship : 'Try me. You won't get by me. In fact, I'll probably hit you for four.' In conversation with anyone so decisive and sharp-witted, it is often a pleasure to be hit for four.

Before leaving that 1963 visit to Australia I must add an onlooker's postscript to Ray Robinson's summary. From my seat in a stand as an England supporter, no Australian fast bowler—McDonald, Gregory, Lindwall, Keith Miller, even Lillee—ever put the wind up me as Alan Davidson did. I have never seen an opening spell so shattering and, to judge from observation, unplayable, as Davidson's in one of these matches. And not only in that match. No fast bowler in Tests against England ever kept my behind so agitated in its seat. Simply a viewer's impersonal estimate. I have never met Davidson to tell him what I thought of him : I wish I had.

Far from impersonal is my estimate of another celebrated Australian bowler. As I have already said, Arthur Mailey was one of my two greatest friends in the world of cricket or in all the rest of the world for that matter (the other one was Raymond Robertson-Glasgow). Experts (notably Ian Peebles) have assessed Mailey's capabilities as a spin bowler, but from what Arthur told me himself, I can appreciate and admire his whole approach to the job. If his Test career results (99 wickets at an average of 33.91) don't appear all that startling, this is largely because he had a perfectly sincere and humorous disdain for figures. What he particularly enjoyed was to baffle a well-set batsman and get him to play a false stroke. But he didn't attempt to cash in on this at once. He would feed the batsman with an innocuous over or two and restore his confidence by presenting him with a couple of nice boundaries before slipping in the baffler again. He got many wickets this way and if, perchance, when the batsman fell for it, the catch was missed, Arthur would enjoy a glow of secret, tight-lipped pleasure, whereas most bowlers would have brought a blush to the cheek of any umpire, however hardened. Arthur would have felt that he at least had got him. Too bad the chance went astray but he'd got what he was out for. He was cricket's greatest philosopher.

Indeed, he was all Australia's greatest philosopher. He had a perfect, quiet sense of values and the sense of humour which prompted it. Samples of his wit have become so widely circulated in cricket circles that I need not repeat them. On the field he kept his humorous reflections to himself, never openly critical of anybody who antagonised him. He just chuckled and let him get on with it and, if the antagonist got the better of him—he just chuckled again. By nature he was a debunker but a completely inoffensive one. It was from some humble artisan job that he emerged to bowl against England and both teams were invited to a reception at Government House in Sydney. The wife of His Excellency chose to be somewhat patronising : 'I suppose this is your first visit to Government House, Mr Mailey.' 'No, ma'am, it isn't. I was here for a while last year. I came to fix the gas."

He was generous by instinct. Once at Lord's I asked him to come along and join me and a couple of girl-friends for lunch. His reply was hearty and spontaneous : 'Fine, Ben. I'll bring the champagne and you get the pies.'

All through the last fifty years of my life my devotion to cricket has only been fostered and animated by my devotion to this whimsical, imperturbable, one-and-only character.

R. C. Robertson-Glasgow (universally addressed and spoken of as 'Crusoe' ever since, in his Oxford days, he dismissed Charles McGahey, of Essex, who deplored being bowled out by Robinson Crusoe) was a complete contrast to Mailey. His outlook on things in general, and cricket in particular, was prompted by a spirit of unsuppressed, thigh-slapping glee. This was apparent in his exceptional talent as a cricket-writer and reporter. He was, in his day, a vigorous fast bowler but met with very moderate success. Once, when he had spent an exhausting and unprofitable morning against Hobbs and Sandham at the Oval, he paused on his way up the pavilion steps to issue his brief confidential report : 'It's like trying to bowl to God on concrete.' He became such a bosom friend of mine because, greatly as we loved the game, we were both always on the look-out for the funny side of it.

One evening in my Somerset home while my two sons were still boys, Crusoe and I were playing that delightful game, stub-cricket with them. When the boys had been bribed to bed, he and I hit on the idea of playing a stub match between England and a team composed of notable figures in the world's history whom we would relish to watch in opposition. Between us we selected a tantalising miscellany. The opening batsmen were St John the Baptist and Beethoven. (Beethoven was run out for nought, being stone deaf and failing to hear a call for a quick single until it was too late.) Among other members of the side were Attila the Hun (fast bowler), Torquemada (spin and googlie expert), Landru (the French bluebeard) and, as wicket-keeper, Mrs Hemans, the poetess—a capricious selection on Crusoe's part. I weighed in with an appropriate pair of umpires—Pontius Pilate and Judge Jeffreys. The test of any great institution such as cricket is that it can survive and absorb ridicule.

Six

Close of Play

I set out with the intention of pampering my aged mind by recalling certain England v. Australia matches and certain England and Australian cricket personalities within my own range of experience. Apart from being glued to the television screen whenever the occasion arises, my cricket watching days are now limited to an annual votive pilgrimage to Canterbury Week. Here my kind hostess, Jane Armitage, a Yorkshire-woman, has inherited and maintained a close association with her county's cricket and one result of this was that I spent an evening at her house with Ray Illingworth. I had often seen him play for England (to open the batting for England in one match). Brian Johnston in his book, *It's a Funny Game*, makes an analytic detailed assessment of all the England captains from Yardley to Brearley and in his final estimate Illingworth tops the lot. A few hours' discussion with Illingworth leaves you with the impression that Brian Johnston undoubtedly knows what he's talking about.

I love these Canterbury days when I meet up again with Leslie Ames, Colin Cowdrey, Jim Swanton and that remark-able wicket-keeper of the distant past, W. H. ('Hopper') Levett. In his time he kept for England, though never against Australia, and he used to stand up to the wicket against fast bowlers. No doubt he would be prepared to do the same today if accom-modated with a pair of stilts.

Leaving aside the limitations which I have imposed upon myself it is possible, perhaps, that some general opinions of a simple spectator, who has observed the game over eighty-five years, may interest other devotees and incense some ('poor old fool'). If so, here are a few of my own personal views for what they are worth.

The really great batsmen fall into two categories. One comes to the wicket saying to the bowlers : 'I am going to slaughter you.' The other comes to the wicket saying : 'You can't get me out.' Don Bradman must rank as the greatest slaughterer on record, Jack Hobbs as the ace 'You-can't get-me-outer'. There are, of course, many who could adapt themselves to prevailing circumstances, no one better at this than Hobbs himself; but I am concerned with the definite, preconceived approach in a batsman's nature. Of the defenders, apart from the Arthur Shrewsburys and W. G. Quaifes of bygone years, we have Phil Mead, Woodfull, Lawry and many others, our Geoffrey Boycott perhaps being the best example of all. In the top class natural attackers from Jessop to Colin Milburn and Botham, there have been many more and it is fun listing for oneself all the greatest exponents (we have already caught a glimpse of Charlie Macartney padded up and snarling assault). I once put this conclusion of mine about the two natural categories to Don Bradman, who commented that he had never heard it put that way before but that I was dead right.

But the batsmen who have given me the greatest delight to watch are not necessarily the slaughterers and certainly not the stern resisters, unless they are having to deal with good spin bowling on a nasty wicket. What, above all, has always appealed to me in batsmanship is style.

In my young days R. H. Spooner was always held up as a model but I saw him only two or three times and never for long. I have mentioned Alan Kippax and I solemnly declare that he gave me more pleasure to watch than any batsman I have ever seen. His immaculate appearance, with those shirt cuffs turned up just above the wrists, seemed to go with the silken elegance of his grace in batsmanship. One of far lesser status, Gerald Crutchley, of Harrow and Middlesex, possessed nearly the same qualities and I always nursed a special admiration for the style of Reginald Simpson, of Nottinghamshire and England. Peter

May must, of course, rank with the elect. His high bat-lift was wont to give me a bit of a tremor but the bat invariably came down in time to perfect the beauty of his stroke-play. Peter May's premature retirement from the game and his self-efface-ment seem to have resulted in his having been somewhat mis-prized (to this watcher, anyhow) as England's greatest batsman since the war.

Another type of batsman who has brought joy and, as it were, comic relief to me, is of the rare type whose bubbling-over confidence takes the form of occasionally cheeking the bowler by producing strokes that are in nobody's book but his own. Denis Compton was the superlative artist in this field, with George Gunn and Pat Hendren just as full of beans if rather less adroit. If I had not been dealing throughout with English and Australian representatives, I would summon Rohan Kanhai to provide further entertainment in this depart-ment.

But I have concerned myself only with my own individual experiences and acquaintances, nearly all of them relating to bygone times, and, so far as the acquaintanceships go, all of them Anglo-Australian, except for two valued New Zealanders, Walter Hadlee and Martin Donnelly. However, this does not mean that I have not spent countless days, over the past fifty years, spellbound and at times almost incredulous watching some of the greatest performances of some of the greatest cricketers in the history of the game, hailing from the rest of the world. But I have never known one of them, except through my field glasses (still the same reliable pair borrowed by Walter Hammond) and it is outside the limitations of this modest effort to begin swopping with my fellow cricket lovers my favourite names on that stupendous list. Nevertheless, they will probably share my sad reflection that at the present moment only two Australians, Greg Chappell and Lillee, could contend for a place in a current world team. As for poor old England, Boycott? I doubt that he'd make it. Even the ebullient Botham might be left to carry the drinks. Needless to say, R. W. Taylor, the best and most cold-shouldered wicket-keeper in the world, would again be ignored.

I am just the old zealot, hobnobbing with his other old and young votaries, to meet with sharp agreement or compassionate scorn. As such, two particular examples of my own freakish picking and choosing, past and present, pop up out of nowhere and everywhere. Both concern the 'rest-of-the-worlders' whom I have vowed to honour in praises unsung. In 1955 and again in 1960 I watched a South African bowler with the most beautiful, flawless, flowing action since Lockwood. He was Neil Adcock. And now, today, if I were given my choice of watching any batsman alive and stroke-making I would plump for Javed Miandad. Knock me down or, in the latter case, better still, wait and see.

And one more 'rest-of-the-worlder'. There can be no controversy about this, anyhow. The greatest all-rounder in the history of the game has been Garfield Sobers. Sir Garfield Sobers —he rather put paid to Arthur Mailey's historical wisecrack when Hutton was honoured: 'Sir Jack Hobbs, Sir Donald Bradman, Sir Leonard Hutton, why must they always be batsmen? The only bowler who ever got to be a knight was Sir Francis Drake.'